# The Psychology of Serial Killers

*Inside the Mind of Monsters and Patterns of Predation*

Scott R. Vanderbilt

# Table of Contents

Introduction ..... 3
Chapter 1: The Dark Fascination ..... 5
Chapter 2: Defining the Monster ..... 13
Chapter 3: The Seeds of Darkness ..... 22
Chapter 4: The Predatory Mind ..... 31
Chapter 5: Hunting Grounds ..... 40
Chapter 6: The Killers' MO ..... 49
Chapter 7: Twisted Motives ..... 58
Chapter 8: Inside Infamous Minds ..... 67
Chapter 9: The Role of Society ..... 77
Chapter 10: The Science of Detection ..... 88
Chapter 11: Inside the Interview Room ..... 99
Chapter 12: The Aftermath ..... 110
Chapter 13: Can Monsters Be Made? ..... 120
Chapter 14: Preventing the Next Monster ..... 131
Conclusion: Reflections on the Human Psyche ..... 142
References ..... 144
About the Author ..... 148
Disclaimer ..... 151
Copyright ..... 152
Legal Notice ..... 153

# Introduction

## A Glimpse into the Abyss

Imagine waking up in the dead of night, your skin prickling with unease. Somewhere in the shadows beyond your home, a predator watches, calculating, waiting. They don't look like monsters. In fact, they could be the friendly neighbor who waves at you every morning, the charming coworker who lingers a little too long in conversation, or the stranger whose smile seems just a bit too practiced. Beneath their carefully crafted masks lies a chilling truth—an insatiable hunger for control, chaos, and blood.

Serial killers are the dark side of human nature personified. They haunt our worst nightmares while living among us in plain sight. How does a person come to be this way? What transforms a seemingly ordinary individual into a calculating predator capable of unspeakable acts? These are the questions that have gripped humanity for centuries, driving us to peer into the abyss of their minds, hoping to understand the unfathomable. And yet, as we learn more, the fear deepens—because the answers are never simple, and the darkness is closer than we think.

In this book, The Psychology of Serial Killers: Inside the Mind of Monsters and Patterns of Predation, we will step into the twisted labyrinth of the killer's psyche. You will uncover what motivates them, how they stalk their prey, and why their horrifying acts resonate so deeply with our primal fears. We will dissect the chilling cases of notorious killers, from their early warning signs to their meticulous methods of manipulation, murder, and mayhem. And as we explore the patterns they leave behind, we will also reveal the humanity—or inhumanity—that lies within.

But be warned: this journey is not for the faint of heart. What you will find here is not just the study of serial killers but a reflection of our shared fragility as humans. It is a deep dive into the shadows of society, where the monsters wear human faces, and evil is more calculated than chaotic.

So, if you dare, turn the page and take the first step into this dark and fascinating world. But keep one thing in mind—what you learn here might change how you see the people around you forever. The real horror isn't in the monsters themselves, but in how easily they can hide among us.

The question is: are you ready to look into the abyss? Because once you do, it will stare back at you.

# Chapter 1: The Dark Fascination

## Why Are We Obsessed with Serial Killers?

Serial killers occupy a peculiar space in the collective psyche of humanity, simultaneously repelling and captivating us. They are the embodiment of our deepest fears and yet, paradoxically, they also ignite a morbid curiosity that keeps us coming back for more. From bestselling books and blockbuster films to true crime podcasts that dominate the airwaves, the stories of serial killers fascinate us in ways few other subjects can. But what is it about these individuals that draws us in so irresistibly?

Part of the allure lies in the mystery they represent. Serial killers exist outside the boundaries of normal human behavior, defying the moral codes that guide society. They provoke questions we cannot easily answer: What compels someone to commit such heinous acts? Were they born this way, or were they shaped by their environment? The enigma of their motivations and the cold precision of their actions create an irresistible puzzle, one that invites us to search for answers no matter how unsettling they may be.

Media plays a significant role in feeding our obsession. The coverage of serial killers often emphasizes their cunning, their ability to evade capture, and the gruesome nature of their crimes. They are portrayed as almost superhuman, their intelligence and audacity exaggerated to mythic proportions. This sensationalism distorts reality but also heightens our fascination. When we consume these stories, whether through news reports or dramatized series, we are engaging with a version of reality that feels larger than life, where the stakes are as high as they can get: life and death.

Psychologically, our interest in serial killers taps into a primal survival instinct. By studying their behavior, we attempt to understand the danger they represent, as if arming ourselves with knowledge could help us recognize and avoid such predators in real life. It's a macabre form of preparation, rooted in the evolutionary drive to protect ourselves and our communities. In this sense, our curiosity about serial killers isn't just morbid—it's an unconscious strategy for staying safe.

There's also a voyeuristic thrill in peering into the darkness without stepping into it ourselves. Serial killers operate on the fringes of morality, breaking rules that most of us wouldn't dare to violate. Observing their actions from a distance allows us to explore the forbidden corners of the human experience while maintaining the safety of detachment. It's like pressing our faces against the glass of a darkened room: we want to see what's inside, but we don't want to be part of it.

Another layer of fascination comes from the idea that serial killers are often ordinary on the surface. They blend into society, holding down jobs, maintaining relationships, and presenting themselves as unremarkable. This duality—the juxtaposition of normalcy and monstrosity—forces us to confront an unsettling truth: evil can hide in plain sight. It challenges our assumptions about trust, safety, and the people around us, making us question just how well we know even those closest to us.

Finally, serial killers reflect the extremes of human potential. While their actions are horrifying, they also reveal the darker capacities of the human mind. They show us what happens when empathy is stripped away, when control becomes obsession, and when the line between fantasy and reality is erased. By studying them, we gain insights not only into their twisted psyches but also into the human condition itself. Serial killers force us to confront uncomfortable truths about our own nature—the impulses we suppress, the fantasies we deny, and the fragile barriers that separate us from chaos.

Our fascination with serial killers, then, is not as simple as morbid curiosity. It's a complex blend of fear, intrigue, and the desire to understand the incomprehensible. They are mirrors that reflect both the darkest corners of society and the vulnerabilities of the human spirit. And as unsettling as that reflection may be, we can't seem to look away.

## Media sensationalism and its impact on the perception of serial killers

Media sensationalism has profoundly shaped public perception of serial killers, often transforming them from dangerous criminals into macabre celebrities. The relentless coverage of their crimes, trials, and personal histories creates an aura of fascination that both horrifies and captivates audiences. This sensationalism doesn't just inform; it dramatizes, embellishes, and amplifies the narrative, distorting how society understands these individuals and their crimes.

One of the most significant impacts of media sensationalism is the creation of mythic personas around serial killers. They are often portrayed as larger-than-life figures, their intelligence and cunning exaggerated to almost superhuman levels. Headlines focus on their ability to outsmart law enforcement, their audacious methods, and the sheer horror of their crimes. This portrayal not only makes them seem more fascinating but also elevates them to a level of notoriety that overshadows their victims and the devastating effects of their actions.

The focus on the grisly details of their crimes further fuels public fascination. Media outlets often highlight the most shocking and gruesome aspects of a case, feeding into the public's appetite for the sensational. This approach turns real-life tragedies into something akin to entertainment, blurring the lines between fact and fiction. The focus on gore and spectacle draws viewers in but rarely contributes to a deeper understanding of the underlying issues, such as mental illness, societal influences, or systemic failures that may have allowed these crimes to continue.

Sensationalized media coverage also skews public perception of who serial killers are and how they operate. By focusing on the most notorious cases—those involving charismatic or particularly violent offenders—media creates a stereotype of the "typical" serial killer. In reality, serial killers come from diverse backgrounds, and their methods and motivations are far more varied than the media often suggests. This oversimplification can lead to misconceptions, making it harder for the public and even law enforcement to recognize other patterns of serial predation.

Another significant impact is the glamorization of serial killers through films, documentaries, and even merchandise. Movies and TV series often present them as enigmatic antiheroes, emphasizing their charm, intelligence, or unique quirks. This glamorization can romanticize their actions, making them appear more intriguing than monstrous. In some cases, it even inspires a subculture of fans who idolize these killers, writing them letters in prison, creating fan art, and treating them as pop culture icons. This phenomenon detracts from the suffering of the victims and perpetuates a twisted fascination with violence.

The victims of serial killers are often relegated to the background in sensationalized coverage. Their lives, stories, and humanity are overshadowed by the media's obsession with the killer. This not only dehumanizes the victims but also reinforces the narrative that the killer's story is the one worth telling. Families of victims frequently speak out against this imbalance, highlighting how the media's focus on the killer prolongs their pain and shifts attention away from justice and healing.

Sensationalism can also influence public fear and policy. Overblown coverage of serial killers can create a sense of widespread danger, even though these crimes are statistically rare. This fear can lead to moral panics and pressure on law enforcement to produce results quickly, which may result in rushed investigations or wrongful convictions. Moreover, the public's skewed perception of serial killers as a pervasive threat can detract from addressing other, more common forms of violent crime.

In the end, media sensationalism often transforms the horrifying reality of serial killers into a spectacle designed to captivate audiences and generate profit. While it's natural for society to seek understanding of such incomprehensible acts, sensationalized coverage prioritizes drama over truth, entertainment over education. This not only distorts public perception but also risks trivializing the profound human suffering left in the wake of these crimes. Recognizing this dynamic is essential if we are to approach the subject of serial killers with the seriousness and respect it demands.

**The cultural allure of the "mind of a monster**

The cultural allure of the "mind of a monster" lies in its ability to both horrify and intrigue, drawing us into the darkest corners of human behavior. Serial killers, often referred to as "monsters" in both media and public discourse, represent a profound deviation from societal norms. Their actions defy logic, morality, and humanity, making them objects of both fear and fascination. This paradox—our simultaneous repulsion and curiosity—has turned the exploration of their minds into a cultural phenomenon.

At its core, the allure stems from our need to understand the incomprehensible. Serial killers embody the ultimate enigma: human beings capable of acts so cruel and calculated that they seem inhuman. Yet, they often live among us, appearing normal, even charming. This contradiction—a person who can simultaneously blend in and commit unimaginable acts—compels us to ask: What makes them tick? By studying the mind of a monster, we attempt to unravel the mystery of what separates them from the rest of us. It's a search for answers to questions about morality, psychology, and the boundaries of human behavior.

The "mind of a monster" also allows us to confront our own darker impulses from a safe distance. Serial killers act out fantasies that society deems unacceptable, crossing lines most people would never dare approach. This transgression of moral boundaries fascinates us because it reveals what can happen when those boundaries are ignored entirely. Exploring their minds is, in a way, a confrontation with the shadow side of humanity—a side we might deny exists within ourselves. It offers a chance to look into the abyss without becoming part of it, satisfying a deep-seated need to explore the forbidden.

Culturally, the fascination with the monstrous mind has been amplified by storytelling. From ancient myths about demons and vampires to modern true crime documentaries, society has long been captivated by tales of predators lurking in the shadows. Serial killers have become the real-world embodiment of these mythical monsters, with their psychological complexity providing endless material for analysis. Their minds offer a narrative that feels both real and surreal, making them ideal subjects for stories that blend fear, intrigue, and a quest for understanding.

The allure is also tied to the idea of control and survival. By dissecting the minds of serial killers, we believe we can protect ourselves. If we understand how they think, perhaps we can recognize the warning signs, avoid dangerous situations, or identify patterns that could help law enforcement. This quest for knowledge is rooted in a survival instinct, a primal need to understand predators to defend against them. The process of exploring the "mind of a monster" becomes a way of reclaiming power in the face of an uncontrollable threat.

Another cultural factor is the elevation of serial killers to near-mythic status. Media, literature, and cinema often portray them as hyper-intelligent masterminds or as deeply tormented figures whose actions stem from tragic origins. This framing humanizes them in ways that make their minds even more intriguing. We are drawn to the duality of their existence—monsters who are also human. This tension between their inhuman acts and their human nature adds depth to their stories, making them compelling subjects for endless analysis and speculation.

Ultimately, the cultural allure of the "mind of a monster" is a reflection of our own need to understand the extremes of human potential. Serial killers push the boundaries of what we think is possible, revealing the darkest capacities of the human psyche. By exploring their minds, we are not only seeking answers about them but also grappling with questions about ourselves. What separates the ordinary from the monstrous? How fragile is the line between good and evil? These are the questions that keep us captivated, drawing us into the minds of monsters in a quest for understanding that is as unsettling as it is irresistible.

# Chapter 2: Defining the Monster

**What Makes a Serial Killer?**

Serial killers are among the most enigmatic and chilling figures in society, individuals who seem to defy the norms of humanity with their actions. To understand what makes a serial killer, one must delve into the intricate web of characteristics and psychological profiles that define these individuals. While no two serial killers are exactly alike, patterns emerge in their behaviors, motivations, and mindsets, providing a framework for defining the "monster" within.

One of the most striking characteristics of serial killers is their ability to compartmentalize their lives. They often present themselves as ordinary, even charming individuals, successfully maintaining jobs, relationships, and social connections. This duality—appearing normal while hiding a darker, predatory side—allows them to evade detection for extended periods. It is this façade of normalcy that makes them so dangerous and difficult to identify, as they blend seamlessly into the very communities they terrorize.

Psychologically, serial killers exhibit traits often associated with psychopathy or sociopathy, though not all of them fit neatly into these categories. A common thread is their lack of empathy, an inability to feel compassion or remorse for their victims. This emotional detachment enables them to commit horrific acts without experiencing guilt or regret. Instead, many serial killers derive pleasure or a sense of control from their crimes, feeding an internal drive that compels them to kill repeatedly.

Another defining trait is the presence of a specific modus operandi (MO) and, in some cases, a ritualistic pattern. The MO refers to the methods and techniques a killer uses to commit their crimes, which can evolve over time as they refine their approach. Rituals, on the other hand, are symbolic or repetitive behaviors that hold personal significance for the killer. These rituals often provide psychological gratification, allowing them to relive their crimes through fantasy and memory. Together, the MO and rituals form a unique "signature" that can help law enforcement link crimes to a specific individual.

Many serial killers also exhibit a profound need for power and control, both over their victims and their environment. This desire often stems from feelings of inadequacy, rejection, or humiliation experienced earlier in life. Killing becomes a way to assert dominance and reclaim a sense of agency, transforming their victims into objects through which they can exert their will. For some, the act of murder is not just about the physical act but about the psychological satisfaction of playing god, deciding who lives and who dies.

The psychological profiles of serial killers also reveal a deep connection to fantasy. Long before they commit their first murder, many serial killers engage in elaborate fantasies that revolve around violence, dominance, or revenge. These fantasies often escalate over time, blending with reality and driving the individual to act on their imagined scenarios. This blurring of fantasy and reality is a critical component of their psychological makeup, as it provides the framework for their crimes.

Early warning signs, often referred to as the "Macdonald Triad," can sometimes be observed in childhood. These signs include persistent bedwetting, cruelty to animals, and fire-setting. While not all serial killers exhibit these behaviors, they are considered potential indicators of underlying psychological issues that may manifest later in life. Childhood trauma, such as abuse, neglect, or exposure to violence, is another common factor, creating a foundation for the distorted thinking and emotional detachment seen in many serial killers.

Despite these shared characteristics, it is important to note that serial killers are not a monolithic group. Their motivations, methods, and psychological profiles vary widely. Some kill for pleasure or sexual gratification, others for revenge, and some for the thrill of evading capture. Understanding these distinctions is crucial for accurately profiling and apprehending them. By studying their shared traits alongside their unique motivations, we can begin to define the "monster" within, not as a singular entity but as a complex and multifaceted phenomenon. This exploration not only helps to identify and stop these predators but also sheds light on the darkest corners of the human mind, challenging us to confront the thin line between order and chaos.

## Differentiating between mass murderers, spree killers, and serial killers

The terms "mass murderer," "spree killer," and "serial killer" are often used interchangeably in popular discourse, but they describe distinct criminal behaviors with key differences in motivation, methodology, and timing. Understanding these distinctions is essential to accurately categorize such crimes and develop strategies for prevention, profiling, and investigation.

A mass murderer is an individual who kills multiple people in a single event or location, typically over a short period. Their crimes are characterized by a concentrated and often indiscriminate burst of violence, targeting multiple victims simultaneously. Mass murders frequently occur in public places such as schools, workplaces, or crowded events, and the perpetrators often end their rampages by taking their own lives or being killed by law enforcement. The motivations for mass murderers vary, but they often stem from personal grievances, ideological extremism, or feelings of powerlessness. Examples include school shooters and perpetrators of workplace violence. Unlike serial killers, their focus is not on the process of killing but on achieving a singular, devastating act that commands attention.

In contrast, a spree killer is defined by their rapid succession of killings across multiple locations without a cooling-off period between events. Spree killers embark on a continuous rampage, moving from one site to another, leaving a trail of victims in their wake. Their attacks can last hours or days, but the lack of a significant pause between killings differentiates them from serial killers. Spree killers are often driven by intense emotional distress, such as anger, desperation, or a sense of hopelessness. Their actions are typically impulsive and chaotic, fueled by a breakdown in rationality rather than the premeditated planning seen in serial killers. Notable spree killing cases often reveal individuals who feel cornered by life circumstances and resort to violence as a form of release or retaliation.

A serial killer, however, operates with a completely different framework. Serial killers commit multiple murders over an extended period, often weeks, months, or even years. What distinguishes them most is the presence of a "cooling-off period" between killings. This interval allows them to return to their daily lives, blending into society while they plan their next crime. Serial killers are methodical and deliberate, often driven by deep psychological compulsions rather than sudden emotional outbursts. They may target specific types of victims or follow a ritualistic pattern, gaining psychological satisfaction from the process of killing. Their crimes are premeditated and often escalate in complexity as they refine their methods over time. Unlike mass murderers or spree killers, serial killers enjoy the act itself and may even relive their crimes through souvenirs, fantasies, or media coverage.

Another critical difference lies in the relationship to their victims. Mass murderers and spree killers often target individuals randomly or based on situational proximity, while serial killers are more selective. Serial killers frequently choose victims who fit a particular profile or fantasy, tailoring their methods to maximize personal gratification. This calculated approach makes serial killers especially difficult to apprehend, as their crimes often appear unconnected and occur in different jurisdictions.

The motivations behind these crimes also vary significantly. While mass murderers often act out of a sense of revenge or ideological conviction, spree killers are typically driven by impulsive rage or a desire to escape perceived injustices. Serial killers, on the other hand, are motivated by psychological gratification, such as a need for power, control, or sexual pleasure. Their actions are deeply personal, rooted in fantasies that shape their behaviors long before their first murder.

Understanding these distinctions is not just a matter of semantics—it is crucial for law enforcement, forensic psychologists, and criminologists. Each type of killer requires different investigative approaches and preventive strategies. Mass and spree killings demand immediate intervention and crisis management, while serial killings necessitate long-term profiling, pattern recognition, and collaboration across jurisdictions. By differentiating between these types of killers, we can gain deeper insights into their motivations and methods, ultimately improving the ability to predict, prevent, and respond to such crimes.

## The FBI's classification and investigative approach

The FBI's classification and investigative approach to serial killers is rooted in decades of research, psychological profiling, and advancements in forensic science. Recognizing the unique nature of serial crimes, the FBI developed specialized strategies to identify patterns, understand motivations, and apprehend offenders. At the heart of this approach is the Behavioral Analysis Unit (BAU), which focuses on studying and profiling offenders to predict their next moves and narrow down suspects.

One of the foundational elements of the FBI's methodology is its classification of serial killers into two broad categories: organized and disorganized. Organized killers are meticulous planners who carefully select their victims, often based on specific characteristics or fantasies. They are methodical in their approach, ensuring minimal evidence is left behind and often staging crime scenes to mislead investigators. These killers typically exhibit higher levels of intelligence and are socially competent, allowing them to blend into society and avoid suspicion. Disorganized killers, on the other hand, act impulsively, with little to no planning involved. Their crimes are often chaotic, driven by emotional or psychological turmoil. They are more likely to leave evidence at the scene due to a lack of forethought or control, making them easier to apprehend than their organized counterparts. This classification helps investigators understand the mindset and behaviors of the offender, shaping the direction of the investigation.

The FBI also emphasizes victimology—the study of the victims—to gain insights into the killer's motives and methods. By analyzing who the victims were, how they were chosen, and the nature of their interactions with the killer, investigators can develop theories about the offender's psychological state, preferred targets, and potential connections to the victims. Victimology also helps identify patterns that can link seemingly unrelated crimes, a critical step in serial killer investigations.

Another cornerstone of the FBI's approach is criminal profiling, a technique that combines psychological analysis with crime scene evidence to create a behavioral and demographic profile of the killer. This profile includes details such as the offender's likely age, gender, occupation, personality traits, and habits. Profiling is particularly valuable in narrowing down suspect pools and predicting the killer's future actions. It allows law enforcement to anticipate where and how the killer might strike again, enabling proactive measures to prevent further crimes.

The FBI's investigative approach also heavily relies on forensic evidence. Advances in DNA analysis, fingerprinting, and digital forensics have revolutionized the ability to link crimes and identify offenders. In cases of serial killings, where offenders often leave behind minimal evidence, even the smallest trace— such as a hair, a fiber, or a fragment of DNA—can be pivotal. The FBI's laboratories and databases, such as CODIS (Combined DNA Index System), play a crucial role in connecting crimes that might otherwise remain unlinked.

Geographic profiling is another tool used by the FBI to track serial killers. By mapping the locations of the crimes, investigators can identify patterns in the offender's movements and narrow down their likely base of operations. This method is especially effective for organized killers, who often operate within a defined geographic area and exhibit predictable behaviors tied to their comfort zones.

Inter-agency collaboration is a critical component of the FBI's strategy. Serial killers often cross state lines, making it necessary for local, state, and federal law enforcement agencies to work together. The Violent Criminal Apprehension Program (ViCAP) was established to facilitate this collaboration. ViCAP is a national database that collects and analyzes information about violent crimes, helping to identify patterns and connect crimes across jurisdictions. This system ensures that vital information is shared among agencies, preventing the killer from exploiting gaps in communication.

In addition to these technical and analytical approaches, the FBI also studies the psychology of serial killers through interviews and case studies. By speaking directly with apprehended killers, investigators gain valuable insights into their thought processes, motivations, and methods. These interviews have contributed significantly to the FBI's understanding of serial killers, shaping the profiles and investigative strategies used today.

The FBI's classification and investigative approach is a multifaceted system designed to address the complexities of serial crimes. By combining behavioral analysis, forensic science, victimology, and inter-agency collaboration, the FBI has developed a robust framework for identifying, understanding, and capturing serial killers. This comprehensive approach not only enhances the likelihood of apprehending offenders but also deepens our understanding of the darkest aspects of human behavior.

# Chapter 3: The Seeds of Darkness

**Early Warning Signs**

The transformation of an individual into a serial killer is rarely spontaneous; it often begins with subtle, yet troubling, behaviors that emerge in childhood or adolescence. These early warning signs, referred to as precursors to violence, provide a glimpse into the psychological and emotional turmoil that can set the stage for future crimes. Among these red flags, the "Macdonald Triad" has garnered significant attention as a framework for identifying potential risk factors. This triad, consisting of persistent bedwetting, arson, and animal cruelty, has been studied extensively for its connection to violent tendencies later in life.

Bedwetting, or enuresis, is the first component of the Macdonald Triad. While bedwetting itself is common among children and often resolves without issue, persistent enuresis beyond the typical developmental years can point to deeper psychological issues. For some individuals, chronic bedwetting becomes a source of shame and humiliation, especially if met with harsh punishment or ridicule from caregivers. This cycle of humiliation and repression can foster feelings of anger, inadequacy, and resentment, emotions that may manifest in destructive or violent behaviors as the individual matures.

Arson, the second component of the triad, represents an escalation in destructive tendencies. Fire-setting is often a means for children or adolescents to express anger, exert control, or channel feelings of powerlessness. The act of watching something burn can provide a sense of dominance over their environment, temporarily alleviating feelings of helplessness or frustration. For some, arson becomes a gateway behavior, offering a thrill that fuels a desire to exert even greater control over life and death.

Animal cruelty, the most concerning element of the Macdonald Triad, is a chilling indicator of a lack of empathy and the emergence of sadistic tendencies. Children who harm animals often do so as a way to project their own feelings of powerlessness onto a vulnerable target. They may derive satisfaction from inflicting pain, exploring a disturbing sense of power over a living creature. This behavior is especially alarming because it suggests a detachment from the suffering of others—a critical psychological component of many serial killers. Studies have shown that individuals who harm animals in childhood are significantly more likely to escalate to harming humans later in life.

While the Macdonald Triad provides a useful framework, it is not a definitive predictor of violent behavior. Many children who exhibit one or more of these behaviors never grow up to become serial killers, and not all serial killers display these warning signs in their youth. However, the triad is often accompanied by other developmental red flags that deepen its significance. For instance, childhood abuse, whether physical, emotional, or sexual, is a common factor in the histories of many violent offenders. Abuse not only damages self-esteem but can also distort an individual's understanding of power, control, and relationships, creating fertile ground for violent impulses to take root.

Neglect and social isolation are also critical factors. Children who grow up feeling unloved or invisible may develop feelings of resentment or alienation. Without positive role models or supportive environments, they may struggle to form healthy emotional connections, instead retreating into fantasy worlds where they can exert control and fulfill their desires. Over time, these fantasies can become increasingly violent, bridging the gap between thought and action.

Bullying, too, plays a significant role in shaping future behavior. Many individuals who become serial killers report being tormented or ostracized during their formative years. This experience can lead to a deep sense of humiliation and a desire for revenge, fueling the development of violent fantasies. For some, this desire to "even the score" manifests as an urge to dominate others through intimidation, violence, or murder.

Another developmental red flag is an obsession with death or violence at an early age. Children who display an unusual fascination with gore, murder, or violent media may be exploring darker aspects of their psyche. While such interests are not inherently dangerous, when combined with other risk factors like cruelty or social isolation, they can indicate a trajectory toward destructive behaviors.

The seeds of darkness, then, are often sown early, through a combination of biological predispositions, environmental factors, and personal experiences. While the presence of the Macdonald Triad and other red flags does not guarantee a violent future, these behaviors provide crucial insights into the psychological struggles of at-risk individuals. Identifying and addressing these warning signs early—through intervention, therapy, and support—can make a critical difference in preventing a path toward violence. By understanding these precursors, we can begin to unravel the complex interplay of factors that create the monsters hiding among us.

# The role of childhood trauma, neglect, and abuse

Childhood trauma, neglect, and abuse are among the most significant factors in shaping the psychology of individuals who later engage in violent behavior, including serial killing. The experiences endured during formative years play a crucial role in the development of personality, coping mechanisms, and emotional regulation. For many serial killers, these early years are marked by profound suffering, creating a foundation of unresolved pain, anger, and dysfunction that manifests in their adult lives as extreme violence and deviant behavior.

Trauma in childhood disrupts the natural process of emotional development. Children who experience physical, emotional, or sexual abuse often internalize feelings of worthlessness and powerlessness. These experiences erode their self-esteem, leaving a deep well of anger and resentment that they are unable to process or express in healthy ways. Instead, this emotional turmoil festers, sometimes transforming into a need for control and dominance over others as a way to compensate for their own sense of helplessness. For many serial killers, the act of murder becomes a twisted form of retribution—a way to reclaim the power that was stripped from them during their formative years.

Neglect is another powerful factor in the creation of psychological wounds that can lead to violent behavior. Children who grow up in environments where their basic needs—love, safety, attention—are ignored often develop a deep sense of invisibility and rejection. This neglect can lead to feelings of alienation and emotional numbness, as the child learns to suppress their emotions to cope with their environment. Over time, this detachment from their own feelings can extend to others, creating an inability to empathize. Serial killers often display this lack of empathy, treating their victims as objects rather than human beings. The root of this detachment frequently lies in the emotional void created by neglect.

Sexual abuse is particularly damaging and is a recurring theme in the histories of many violent offenders. Victims of such abuse often grapple with intense shame, confusion, and self-loathing. This trauma can distort their understanding of intimacy and power, as they begin to associate these concepts with control and dominance rather than mutual respect or love. For some, the pain of their own abuse is reenacted in their crimes, as they take on the role of the abuser in an attempt to regain control over their deeply damaged psyche. This cycle of abuse perpetuates the very pain they endured, externalizing their internal torment onto their victims.

The intersection of trauma and fantasy is also a critical aspect of how childhood abuse shapes future behavior. Children who suffer from abuse or neglect often retreat into fantasies as a way to escape their harsh realities. While fantasy can be a healthy coping mechanism in some contexts, for those predisposed to violence, these fantasies can take a darker turn. Over time, the individual may develop elaborate scenarios of revenge, dominance, or control that begin to blend with reality. This blurring of lines between fantasy and real-life action becomes a critical driver for serial killers, who often report fantasizing about their crimes long before committing them.

Attachment theory provides further insight into the role of childhood trauma in shaping future violence. Secure attachment during childhood fosters healthy emotional bonds and the ability to trust others. However, children who experience neglect or abuse often develop insecure or disorganized attachment styles. They may struggle to form meaningful relationships or view others as sources of pain rather than comfort. This distorted perspective on human connection can lead to isolation and an inability to relate to others in a compassionate way. Serial killers often exhibit signs of this detachment, seeing their victims as tools to fulfill their needs rather than as individuals with their own value.

The role of childhood trauma is not just psychological but also neurological. Chronic exposure to abuse, neglect, or violence can alter the developing brain, particularly in regions associated with emotional regulation, impulse control, and empathy. These changes can make individuals more prone to aggression, less capable of controlling violent impulses, and less likely to understand or care about the impact of their actions on others. This biological component adds another layer of complexity to the link between childhood trauma and later violence.

Ultimately, childhood trauma, neglect, and abuse create a perfect storm of psychological and emotional dysfunction that can set the stage for violent behavior. While not all individuals who experience such hardships go on to commit violent acts, these factors are undeniably present in the backgrounds of many serial killers. Understanding the role of early-life experiences in shaping their behavior underscores the importance of intervention, support, and prevention. By addressing these issues in childhood, society has the opportunity to disrupt the cycle of violence before it begins, offering a path toward healing rather than harm.

# Nature vs. nurture: The debate on biology versus environment

The nature vs. nurture debate is one of the most enduring and complex discussions in psychology, particularly when examining the origins of violent behavior, including serial killing. This debate centers on whether biological factors, such as genetics and brain chemistry, or environmental influences, such as upbringing and social experiences, play a more significant role in shaping individuals who commit heinous acts. While both sides offer compelling arguments, research increasingly suggests that the interplay between nature and nurture is what ultimately drives behavior, creating a nuanced picture of how serial killers are made.

The "nature" argument focuses on the role of biology in predisposing individuals to violence. Genetic factors, for example, have been linked to aggressive behavior. Studies of twins and families have shown that certain personality traits, such as impulsivity, low empathy, and a propensity for risk-taking, can have a hereditary component. Specific genes, like the MAOA gene, sometimes referred to as the "warrior gene," have been associated with aggressive behavior, especially when coupled with adverse environmental conditions. Additionally, brain abnormalities, such as dysfunction in the prefrontal cortex or the amygdala, can impair emotional regulation and impulse control, making individuals more likely to engage in violent acts. These biological predispositions provide a foundation for understanding why some people may be more susceptible to developing criminal tendencies.

On the other hand, the "nurture" argument emphasizes the role of environment and experiences in shaping behavior. Childhood trauma, such as abuse, neglect, or exposure to violence, has a well-documented connection to violent tendencies later in life. Social environments, including dysfunctional family dynamics, poverty, and peer influence, also contribute significantly. A child who grows up in an abusive household, for example, may learn that violence is an acceptable way to exert control or resolve conflict. Similarly, a lack of positive role models or support systems can leave individuals ill-equipped to cope with their emotions in healthy ways, pushing them toward destructive behaviors. The nurture perspective underscores that violent behavior is often a learned response to external circumstances rather than an innate trait.

When it comes to serial killers, neither nature nor nurture alone seems sufficient to explain their behavior. Instead, it is the interaction between the two that creates the conditions for their violent tendencies to emerge. For example, an individual may be born with a genetic predisposition toward aggression or emotional detachment, but it is the environment—abuse, neglect, or social isolation—that activates these traits and channels them into violence. This combination of factors helps explain why not everyone with a biological predisposition to aggression becomes a serial killer, and why not everyone who experiences trauma turns to violence. It is the convergence of these elements that sets the stage for such extreme behavior.

The interplay between nature and nurture is also evident in the development of psychological disorders often associated with serial killers, such as antisocial personality disorder (ASPD) or psychopathy. While these disorders may have a biological basis, their expression is influenced by environmental factors. A child with a genetic predisposition to ASPD, for instance, may never develop violent tendencies if raised in a loving and supportive environment. Conversely, a child without such a predisposition may develop similar behaviors if exposed to severe trauma or neglect. This interaction highlights the importance of context in determining how biological traits manifest in behavior.

Research into the nature vs. nurture debate has also revealed that environmental factors can shape biology itself, a concept known as epigenetics. Adverse experiences, such as chronic stress or trauma, can alter the way genes are expressed, effectively "turning on" or "turning off" certain genetic predispositions. This means that an individual's environment can influence not only their behavior but also their biology, further blurring the lines between nature and nurture. For serial killers, this dynamic may help explain why some individuals with seemingly normal upbringings still develop violent tendencies, while others with traumatic pasts do not.

Ultimately, the nature vs. nurture debate is not about choosing one side over the other but about understanding how the two forces interact. Serial killers are not born nor made in isolation; they are the product of a complex interplay between their genetic makeup and the environments in which they are raised. Recognizing this complexity is crucial for developing effective interventions, whether through early detection of at-risk individuals, therapeutic support for trauma survivors, or broader societal efforts to address the root causes of violence. The debate reminds us that human behavior, especially at its extremes, is rarely simple, and understanding it requires examining the intricate relationship between biology and environment.

# Chapter 4: The Predatory Mind

## Understanding the Psychology of Killing

The psychology of serial killers is a labyrinth of darkness, where deviant thought patterns, unresolved trauma, and psychological disorders converge to create individuals capable of unimaginable acts. While no single psychological profile fits all serial killers, certain disorders and personality traits frequently emerge, offering insight into the inner workings of their predatory minds. These disorders and traits form the foundation of their motivations, enabling their capacity to kill repeatedly with chilling detachment or gratification.

One of the most commonly associated psychological disorders in serial killers is antisocial personality disorder (ASPD). Individuals with ASPD exhibit a pervasive disregard for societal norms and the rights of others. They are often manipulative, deceitful, and lacking in empathy, which allows them to view their victims not as people but as objects to be used for their own gain or gratification. This detachment from moral and emotional constraints enables them to commit acts of violence without remorse. ASPD often overlaps with psychopathy, a more severe manifestation characterized by superficial charm, egocentricity, and a complete inability to feel guilt. Many serial killers who have been studied display high levels of psychopathy, allowing them to manipulate their victims and evade detection with calculated precision.

Narcissistic personality traits are also prevalent among serial killers, fueling their sense of superiority and entitlement. Narcissism leads these individuals to believe they are above the rules of society, deserving of power and control over others. This inflated sense of self-worth often drives their desire to dominate and dehumanize their victims, as killing becomes a means of asserting their perceived omnipotence. The combination of narcissism and a lack of empathy creates a dangerous cocktail, where others are seen merely as tools for fulfilling personal fantasies or desires.

Obsessive-compulsive tendencies may also play a role in shaping the behavior of serial killers, particularly in their rituals and methods. Many killers display an intense need for control, meticulously planning their crimes and adhering to specific routines or patterns. These rituals often serve as psychological anchors, providing them with a sense of order and stability in their otherwise chaotic minds. For example, some serial killers may revisit crime scenes, take trophies, or perform specific actions with their victims, all of which are driven by obsessive thoughts that compel them to relive or perfect their crimes.

Another significant factor in the psychology of serial killers is their ability to compartmentalize. This trait allows them to separate their everyday lives from their violent acts, often leading double lives that appear perfectly normal on the surface. This ability to switch between personas enables them to evade suspicion, as they present themselves as charming, hardworking, or even caring individuals in public while harboring a dark and predatory side. Compartmentalization not only protects their secrets but also allows them to rationalize their actions, distancing themselves emotionally from the consequences of their crimes.

Paraphilic disorders, or abnormal sexual desires, are also common in many serial killers, particularly those motivated by lust. These disorders often involve deviant fantasies that blend violence and sexuality, driving their need to act out these fantasies through murder. For these killers, the act of killing is not solely about power or control but also about fulfilling deeply ingrained, distorted desires. The line between fantasy and reality becomes blurred, and the satisfaction they derive from their crimes reinforces their compulsion to kill again.

In addition to these psychological disorders, many serial killers exhibit a profound inability to regulate their emotions. While they may appear calm and calculating, their actions are often driven by underlying anger, frustration, or resentment. This emotional instability can stem from childhood trauma, neglect, or abuse, which leaves deep psychological scars. The inability to process these emotions in healthy ways leads to a buildup of internal tension, which they release through violence. For some, the act of killing provides a temporary sense of relief or empowerment, further reinforcing their behavior.

What sets serial killers apart from other violent offenders is their predatory mindset. They do not act impulsively or in the heat of the moment; instead, their crimes are deliberate and calculated. They often exhibit a "hunting" behavior, selecting victims who fit specific criteria or fulfill their fantasies. This predatory approach reflects their deep need for control, as they manipulate their victims into vulnerable positions before striking. For many, the act of stalking or planning is as gratifying as the murder itself, as it allows them to exert dominance over their chosen prey.

Ultimately, the psychology of serial killers is a complex interplay of disorders, traits, and environmental influences that converge to create individuals capable of repeated violence. Their lack of empathy, compulsive tendencies, emotional detachment, and predatory instincts combine to form a dangerous and chilling profile. By understanding these psychological patterns, we can better recognize, prevent, and respond to the unique threat posed by those with predatory minds.

## The role of psychopathy and sociopathy

Psychopathy and sociopathy are two distinct yet closely related personality disorders that play a central role in understanding the behaviors of many serial killers. Both fall under the broader category of antisocial personality disorder (ASPD), characterized by a disregard for societal norms and a lack of empathy for others. However, the subtle differences between psychopathy and sociopathy provide crucial insights into the motives, methods, and mental states of individuals who engage in serial violence.

Psychopathy is often described as the most extreme manifestation of ASPD. Psychopaths are highly manipulative, emotionally detached, and calculated in their actions. They are masters of deception, often able to mimic normal emotional responses to blend seamlessly into society. This ability to mask their true nature allows them to gain the trust of others, making their predatory actions all the more chilling. Psychopaths typically display a profound lack of empathy, enabling them to view their victims as objects rather than people. This emotional detachment is what allows them to commit heinous acts with no remorse or guilt. Many serial killers with psychopathic traits meticulously plan their crimes, demonstrating a cold, calculating approach that reflects their need for control and dominance.

Sociopathy, on the other hand, is often associated with more impulsive and erratic behavior. Sociopaths, while also lacking empathy, tend to struggle with emotional regulation and are more prone to outbursts of anger or frustration. Unlike psychopaths, who often live double lives and maintain a façade of normalcy, sociopaths may have difficulty forming and maintaining relationships due to their volatile nature. Their crimes are often less organized and more opportunistic, reflecting their impulsive tendencies and inability to think through the consequences of their actions. While psychopaths are driven by a need for power and control, sociopaths are more likely to act out of emotional instability or personal vendettas.

One of the key differences between psychopathy and sociopathy lies in their origins. Psychopathy is believed to have a stronger biological basis, with research suggesting that abnormalities in brain structures like the amygdala and prefrontal cortex contribute to their emotional detachment and lack of impulse control. Sociopathy, on the other hand, is often rooted in environmental factors, such as childhood trauma, neglect, or exposure to violence. Sociopaths are frequently the product of chaotic or abusive environments that distort their understanding of relationships, emotions, and morality. These differences highlight the complex interplay of nature and nurture in shaping individuals with these disorders.

In the context of serial killers, psychopathy is more commonly associated with those who exhibit methodical, ritualistic behavior. Psychopathic killers often display a high degree of organization, stalking their victims and carefully planning their attacks to avoid detection. They may take trophies or revisit crime scenes, deriving pleasure from the memory of their crimes. Their ability to remain calm under pressure and manipulate others often allows them to evade capture for extended periods. Notable examples of psychopathic serial killers include Ted Bundy, who charmed his victims with his good looks and intelligence, only to reveal his true, predatory nature once they were in his control.

Sociopathic serial killers, while less common, exhibit a different pattern of behavior. Their crimes are often driven by emotional outbursts or personal grudges, making them less predictable and more chaotic. They may lack the careful planning and manipulation seen in psychopaths, but their impulsivity and willingness to act on violent urges make them equally dangerous. Sociopaths are also more likely to be caught due to their erratic behavior and inability to cover their tracks effectively. While their lack of organization may seem like a weakness, it also makes them harder to profile, as their actions often lack a clear pattern or motive.

Despite their differences, both psychopathy and sociopathy share the trait of emotional detachment, which is critical in understanding the mindset of serial killers. Neither group experiences guilt or remorse in the same way that most people do, allowing them to commit repeated acts of violence without being weighed down by the psychological burden of their actions. This emotional void is central to their ability to rationalize or even take pleasure in their crimes.

Ultimately, the roles of psychopathy and sociopathy in serial killing underscore the complexity of understanding such extreme behavior. While both disorders contribute to the lack of empathy and moral detachment that enable serial killers to act, the differences in their origins, traits, and behaviors highlight the diverse paths that can lead to such violence. By studying these disorders, researchers and law enforcement professionals can better identify the warning signs, motivations, and methods of individuals with a predisposition toward serial violence, offering critical insights into preventing and solving these crimes.

## How serial killers rationalize and justify their actions

Serial killers often engage in complex mental gymnastics to rationalize and justify their actions, constructing narratives that allow them to reconcile their horrific behavior with their self-perception. These justifications are not merely excuses but are deeply rooted in their psychological makeup, serving as mechanisms to suppress guilt, avoid accountability, and maintain a sense of control. By creating these distorted frameworks, serial killers shield themselves from the moral and emotional weight of their crimes, enabling them to kill repeatedly without remorse.

One common form of rationalization is the dehumanization of victims. Serial killers often view their victims as objects or symbols rather than as people with intrinsic value. This dehumanization allows them to strip their victims of individuality, reducing them to mere tools for achieving their goals or fulfilling their fantasies. For example, some killers see their victims as representatives of a group they despise, such as a particular gender, profession, or social class, and justify their actions as a form of "punishment." By depersonalizing their victims, they create an emotional distance that makes their crimes psychologically tolerable.

Another justification frequently employed by serial killers is the belief that they are serving a higher purpose. Some frame their actions as part of a divine mission, a quest for justice, or a means to cleanse society of undesirables. This delusion of moral superiority enables them to view their crimes not as acts of evil but as necessary steps toward a larger, often imagined, goal. For example, a killer might convince themselves that they are "saving" their victims from suffering or punishing them for perceived sins, transforming their violent actions into what they see as a justified or even noble cause.

A number of serial killers also rationalize their behavior through self-victimization. They view their crimes as a response to the injustices or traumas they have endured in their own lives, positioning themselves as victims who are merely retaliating against an unfair world. This mindset often stems from experiences of childhood abuse, neglect, or bullying, which they perceive as giving them the right to take out their anger and frustration on others. By framing their actions as a form of retribution or emotional release, they shift blame onto external forces, absolving themselves of personal responsibility.

For some killers, rationalization is rooted in their belief that their actions are inevitable. They see themselves as driven by uncontrollable urges or biological imperatives that they cannot resist, convincing themselves that they are simply acting according to their nature. This fatalistic perspective often leads them to accept their behavior as an unavoidable aspect of who they are, allowing them to avoid accountability. By framing their killings as beyond their control, they can commit their crimes without wrestling with the moral implications of their actions.

Ego and narcissism also play a significant role in the justification process. Many serial killers see themselves as superior to others, believing that societal rules and moral codes do not apply to them. This inflated sense of self-worth allows them to view their actions as exceptions to normal human behavior, reinforcing their belief that they are above judgment or consequence. Their arrogance often leads them to see their killings as a demonstration of their power, intelligence, or creativity, further insulating them from feelings of guilt or shame.

In addition, some serial killers justify their actions through a distorted sense of scientific or philosophical reasoning. They may claim to be conducting "experiments" to explore human behavior, life, or death, reframing their crimes as intellectual pursuits rather than acts of violence. This pseudo-scientific rationalization enables them to distance themselves from their actions, portraying themselves as objective observers rather than perpetrators. By intellectualizing their crimes, they can avoid confronting the emotional and moral realities of their behavior.

Ultimately, the ways in which serial killers rationalize their actions reveal the depth of their psychological dysfunction and detachment from societal norms. These justifications are not only tools for avoiding guilt but also serve to sustain their ability to commit repeated acts of violence. By constructing these distorted narratives, they maintain a fragile sense of control over their identities, allowing them to continue their predatory behavior without being consumed by the weight of their actions. Understanding these rationalizations provides critical insight into the inner workings of the predatory mind and the complex mechanisms that enable serial killers to persist in their violent pursuits.

# Chapter 5: Hunting Grounds

## How Serial Killers Select Their Victims

The process by which serial killers select their victims is not random but rather a calculated act shaped by patterns of predation and victimology. Understanding these patterns offers crucial insights into the psychology of serial killers and the strategies they use to target, manipulate, and ultimately overpower their victims. Their choices are influenced by a combination of psychological desires, personal fantasies, and practical considerations, all of which align with their need for control, dominance, or gratification.

At the core of victim selection is the concept of victimology, which examines the characteristics of those targeted by killers. Serial killers often choose victims who fulfill specific criteria that align with their fantasies or desires. For some, the victims symbolize a figure from their past—an abusive parent, a neglectful caregiver, or a former partner. By targeting individuals who evoke these associations, killers attempt to reenact or resolve unresolved emotions tied to their trauma. For others, victims represent a particular type, such as a specific gender, age group, or social status. This selectivity reflects the killer's internal narrative and the psychological needs they seek to fulfill through their crimes.

Patterns of predation often involve meticulous planning and an acute understanding of vulnerability. Serial killers tend to target individuals they perceive as easy to overpower, such as children, the elderly, sex workers, or people living on the margins of society. These groups are often chosen not only because they are physically or socially vulnerable but also because their disappearances are less likely to attract immediate attention. Killers exploit this lack of scrutiny, knowing it provides them with the time and opportunity to act without interference.

The choice of hunting ground is another critical aspect of predation. Serial killers often operate in areas where they feel a sense of control or familiarity, such as their own neighborhoods, places of work, or communities they frequent. These locations, referred to as "comfort zones," allow them to observe potential victims over time, learning their habits and routines. Some killers expand their hunting grounds as they gain confidence, but most remain within a defined geographic area where they feel secure. Geographic profiling, which maps the locations of their crimes, often reveals patterns that can help investigators predict where a killer might strike next.

For many serial killers, the process of selecting a victim involves stalking or observing their target for a period of time. This stalking behavior provides the killer with a sense of control and satisfaction, as they dominate the victim without the latter's awareness. Stalking also allows killers to assess the risk of detection, ensuring they choose the most opportune moment to strike. This predatory behavior mirrors the instincts of hunters in the wild, further emphasizing the primal, calculated nature of their actions.

In some cases, killers rely on lures or manipulative tactics to draw victims into their traps. These methods often involve exploiting the victim's trust or empathy. For example, some killers feign injury or distress to elicit help, using their charm or charisma to disarm their targets. Others pose as authority figures, such as police officers or security personnel, to create a false sense of safety. These manipulative tactics highlight the psychological acumen of many serial killers, who use deception as a weapon to gain access to their victims.

The escalation of predation often reveals an evolution in the killer's methods. Early victims may be chosen based on convenience or opportunity, but as killers refine their techniques, their selection process becomes more deliberate and aligned with their fantasies. This progression reflects their growing confidence and sense of invincibility, which can ultimately lead to mistakes that expose them to law enforcement. The refinement of their methods also underscores the addictive nature of their crimes, as each act pushes them closer to perfecting their twisted desires.

While the patterns of victim selection and predation may vary between killers, one constant is the deep psychological significance these choices hold for them. Every victim represents more than just a target; they are a piece of a larger narrative in the killer's mind, a means to fulfill an emotional void, enact revenge, or assert control. By understanding these patterns, investigators can gain valuable insights into the killer's psyche, motivations, and potential next moves. These insights not only aid in apprehension but also deepen our understanding of the predatory mind, shedding light on the dark and calculated strategies that define the actions of serial killers.

## Understanding the role of fantasy in selecting and targeting victims

Fantasy plays a central role in the behavior of serial killers, serving as the foundation upon which their actions are built. Long before they commit their first murder, many serial killers develop vivid and elaborate fantasies that shape their desires, motivations, and selection of victims. These fantasies are not fleeting thoughts but deeply ingrained narratives that they revisit repeatedly, fine-tuning the details until the line between imagination and reality begins to blur. Understanding the role of fantasy in targeting and selecting victims is critical to comprehending the psychological processes that drive these killers.

For most serial killers, fantasies begin as a way to escape their feelings of powerlessness, inadequacy, or frustration. These mental scenarios provide a sense of control and dominance that is absent in their real lives. Over time, the fantasies become more intricate, focusing on specific scenarios, rituals, or victim types that align with their desires. These imagined narratives create an idealized version of the act of killing, where the killer exerts complete authority over a vulnerable target, fulfilling their need for power, revenge, or gratification.

The victims chosen by serial killers often fit the archetypes established in their fantasies. They may target individuals who resemble a figure from their past—a neglectful parent, an abusive partner, or someone who symbolizes rejection or humiliation. By selecting victims who fit this mold, the killer attempts to resolve unresolved conflicts or replay past traumas with a sense of control. For others, the choice of victims is driven by aesthetic or symbolic elements that align with their fantasies. These preferences can include specific physical features, clothing, or behaviors, all of which serve to reinforce the killer's imagined scenario.

Fantasies also guide the methods and rituals employed by serial killers. Many killers meticulously plan their crimes to match the script in their minds, ensuring that the real-world act mirrors the imagined one as closely as possible. This alignment between fantasy and reality is crucial for the psychological satisfaction they derive from their crimes. When the act deviates from their expectations, it can lead to frustration or an escalation in violence as they attempt to recreate the idealized scenario. This compulsion to relive their fantasies is what drives many serial killers to kill repeatedly, each act serving as an attempt to perfect their imagined narrative.

In the targeting process, fantasy shapes not only the choice of victims but also the methods used to manipulate and capture them. Serial killers often devise elaborate plans to lure victims into situations that align with their imagined scenarios. They may pose as authority figures, use charm to gain trust, or create situations that make their victims feel safe. These tactics are carefully crafted to mirror the dynamics envisioned in their fantasies, allowing the killer to feel a sense of mastery over the situation.

The role of fantasy in victim selection also explains why some serial killers take trophies or revisit crime scenes. These acts allow them to extend the fantasy beyond the moment of the crime, enabling them to relive the experience repeatedly. Trophies serve as physical reminders of their dominance and control, while returning to crime scenes reinforces their sense of power and ownership over their actions. For many killers, the fantasy does not end with the murder; it continues to evolve, feeding their compulsion to kill again.

While fantasy is a driving force, it also creates vulnerabilities that law enforcement can exploit. The consistency of these imagined scenarios often leads to patterns in the killer's behavior, such as specific victim types, methods, or locations. By analyzing these patterns, investigators can gain insights into the killer's psyche, motivations, and likely next moves. Understanding the role of fantasy provides a window into the mind of the offender, helping to predict their behavior and ultimately bring them to justice.

Fantasy is not just a backdrop to the actions of serial killers—it is the blueprint that guides their every move. It shapes who they target, how they approach their crimes, and the satisfaction they derive from their actions. By examining the role of fantasy, we can uncover the deeply rooted psychological mechanisms that drive these individuals, offering a deeper understanding of the forces that compel them to act and the devastating impact of their imagined worlds brought to life.

### Geographic profiling and the "hunting grounds

Geographic profiling is a vital tool in understanding and investigating the patterns of serial killers, particularly in identifying their "hunting grounds." This method of analysis examines the locations of a killer's crimes to uncover patterns and predict their base of operations or future activity. Serial killers rarely act at random; instead, their crimes often occur within areas where they feel comfortable, familiar, or in control. These hunting grounds are central to their predatory behavior, serving as the physical spaces where their fantasies are brought to life.

A killer's hunting ground is typically tied to areas where they have a psychological or practical advantage. This could include their home neighborhood, places of work, or locations they frequently visit. These areas, referred to as comfort zones, offer them a sense of familiarity that reduces the risk of being caught.

Within these zones, they can observe potential victims over time, learning their habits and routines. The comfort and confidence they feel in these areas enhance their ability to plan and execute their crimes with precision.

Geographic profiling focuses on analyzing the spatial patterns of these crimes to create a map of the killer's movements. Investigators use data from crime scenes, body disposal sites, and other locations associated with the killer's activity to identify a "geographic signature." This signature often reveals the boundaries of the killer's comfort zone and provides insight into their routines and behavior. The method relies on the principle that most serial killers operate within a limited geographic area, striking close enough to their base to feel secure but far enough away to avoid drawing attention to themselves.

The concept of distance decay is central to geographic profiling. This principle suggests that the likelihood of committing a crime decreases as the distance from the offender's base of operations increases. Serial killers often follow this pattern, targeting victims in areas that are close enough to their home or workplace to be accessible but not so close as to risk exposure. By analyzing the distribution of crime locations, profilers can estimate the area where the killer is most likely to reside or spend significant time.

There are exceptions to this pattern, particularly among highly organized killers who are willing to travel long distances to avoid detection. These killers may create multiple hunting grounds or operate across different jurisdictions, complicating the investigative process. However, even in these cases, geographic profiling can help identify clusters of activity that point to the killer's preferred environments or travel patterns. This information is crucial in narrowing down suspect pools and allocating investigative resources more effectively.

The choice of hunting grounds is influenced by the killer's psychological needs and logistical considerations. Some killers prefer densely populated urban areas where they can find an abundance of potential victims and remain anonymous in the crowd. Others may target rural or isolated locations where they can act with minimal risk of interruption. The environment itself often plays a role in the killer's fantasies, with some choosing locations that hold personal significance or align with their desired narrative. For example, a killer who fantasizes about control and dominance may favor secluded spots where they have complete control over the crime scene.

Geographic profiling also helps investigators understand the escalation of a killer's activity. Many serial killers begin their crimes within their immediate comfort zones, where they feel safest. As they gain confidence or become more compulsive, they may expand their hunting grounds, venturing further from their base. This expansion can create new patterns that, when analyzed, provide clues about the killer's evolving mindset and behavior.

The importance of hunting grounds extends beyond the physical act of killing. For many serial killers, these locations are carefully chosen to reinforce their sense of power and control. Returning to crime scenes or revisiting familiar hunting grounds can provide them with psychological gratification, allowing them to relive their crimes and feel a renewed sense of dominance. This behavior often creates additional data points for geographic profiling, as these revisits can form part of the larger pattern investigators analyze.

Geographic profiling is not just a practical tool for law enforcement; it also offers profound insights into the psychology of serial killers. Their choice of hunting grounds reflects their need for control, their understanding of risk, and the way their fantasies intersect with the real world. By mapping these patterns, investigators can uncover the invisible boundaries that define a killer's predatory behavior, ultimately bringing them one step closer to apprehension. Understanding the role of hunting grounds highlights the calculated nature of serial killers, emphasizing their deliberate planning and the chilling precision with which they carry out their crimes.

# Chapter 6: The Killers' MO

## Methods, Rituals, and Signatures

The terms "modus operandi" (MO) and "ritualistic behavior" are often used in the context of serial killer investigations, but they represent distinct aspects of a killer's behavior. Both play critical roles in understanding and profiling serial offenders, providing insights into their psychology, motivations, and patterns. While the MO reflects the practical side of their crimes—the "how" of what they do—ritualistic behavior reveals the deeper, more personal and psychological elements that drive their actions.

The modus operandi, or MO, refers to the methods and techniques a killer uses to commit their crimes. It includes everything from how they select their victims to the tools and strategies employed during the act itself. The MO is shaped by the killer's need to successfully complete the crime and avoid detection, making it a practical and functional aspect of their behavior. For instance, some killers use specific lures, like pretending to need help or offering a ride, to gain the trust of their victims. Others rely on specific weapons, locations, or times of day that minimize the risk of being caught. The MO is not static; it often evolves as the killer gains experience, refines their methods, and adapts to challenges or close calls. This evolution reflects the killer's learning process and their ability to improve their "craft" over time.

Ritualistic behavior, on the other hand, is rooted in the killer's psychological needs and fantasies. Rituals are repetitive, often symbolic acts that hold personal significance for the killer but are not necessary for the commission of the crime. These behaviors go beyond the practical elements of the MO and are tied to the killer's internal desires, obsessions, or emotional gratification. For example, a killer may arrange the victim's body in a specific position, leave behind symbolic items, or perform post-mortem actions that reflect their fantasies. Unlike the MO, which can change based on necessity, rituals are more consistent because they are deeply tied to the killer's psychological identity. A disruption in the ritual may leave the killer feeling dissatisfied or compelled to commit another crime to fulfill their fantasy properly.

The distinction between MO and ritualistic behavior is crucial in criminal profiling because it helps investigators understand both the practical and psychological aspects of the crime. The MO reveals how the killer operates, while the ritual exposes why they kill and what drives them. For example, a serial killer might consistently strangle their victims (MO) but also take a lock of hair as a trophy (ritual). The MO reflects their need to efficiently carry out the murder, while the ritual satisfies a deeper psychological compulsion. By analyzing both, profilers can develop a more comprehensive understanding of the killer's mindset and predict future behaviors.

Another important concept related to rituals is the "signature." A signature is a specific aspect of the crime that is unique to the killer and is a direct expression of their fantasies or psychological needs. While rituals can sometimes overlap with the MO, the signature is entirely unnecessary for committing the crime and serves no functional purpose. It is purely symbolic, representing the killer's emotional or psychological imprint on the crime scene. For instance, a killer who leaves behind handwritten notes at every crime scene or arranges objects in a specific pattern is displaying a signature. These unique elements often help law enforcement link crimes together, even when the MO varies.

The interplay between MO, ritual, and signature becomes even more complex as serial killers evolve. While the MO may adapt based on circumstances, the ritual and signature often remain consistent, providing critical clues for investigators. Changes in MO may occur due to increased confidence, the need to avoid detection, or external factors, such as media attention or law enforcement pressure. However, the ritual and signature remain tied to the killer's core psychological makeup, making them more reliable indicators of their identity and motivations.

Understanding the distinction between MO and ritual also highlights the emotional component of serial killings. The MO reflects the practical, goal-oriented side of the killer, while the ritual reveals their need for emotional fulfillment or psychological release. For many killers, the act of murder alone is not enough; it must align with the narrative in their minds, where the ritual plays a central role. This duality underscores the complexity of their behavior, blending calculated pragmatism with deeply rooted psychological drives.

By studying both the MO and ritualistic behaviors of serial killers, investigators can piece together a detailed profile that combines the "how" and "why" of their crimes. This understanding not only aids in connecting seemingly unrelated cases but also provides valuable insights into the predatory mind, ultimately bringing law enforcement closer to identifying and apprehending the offender. The distinction between these elements is more than a technicality—it is a window into the dual nature of serial killers, where methodical precision meets dark, compulsive fantasies.

# The role of escalation in the behavior of serial killers

Escalation is a defining characteristic in the behavior of serial killers, reflecting the gradual intensification of their actions, methods, and psychological needs over time. This process is not simply a matter of increasing violence but rather a complex progression driven by psychological gratification, a growing sense of invincibility, and the compulsion to refine their crimes. Escalation reveals the evolving nature of a serial killer's mindset and provides critical insights into their motivations and patterns.

In the early stages, escalation often begins with fantasies that become increasingly vivid and detailed. Many serial killers start by imagining acts of violence or control, replaying these scenarios in their minds for psychological gratification. Over time, these fantasies become insufficient, and they feel compelled to act them out in the real world. The initial crime often serves as a testing ground, where the killer experiments with methods and victims. This first act is rarely perfect, as the killer learns from mistakes and begins to refine their approach.

As the killer gains experience, their confidence grows, leading to a more methodical and calculated approach. This is where escalation becomes more apparent. The killer may become more daring, targeting victims in public places, expanding their geographic range, or increasing the frequency of their crimes. This progression is often fueled by the psychological high they experience from their actions. The satisfaction they derive from their crimes diminishes over time, requiring them to push boundaries further to achieve the same level of gratification.

Each subsequent crime becomes an attempt to recapture or surpass the thrill of the previous one.

Escalation is also evident in the increasing brutality of the crimes. Many serial killers start with less violent or intrusive methods, such as strangulation, and gradually move to more gruesome acts, including mutilation or torture. This escalation in violence is driven by a need for greater control and dominance over their victims. For some, the act of killing alone is no longer enough; they begin to incorporate rituals, post-mortem actions, or symbolic behaviors that align with their fantasies. This intensification often reflects the killer's deepening psychological compulsions and their need to assert complete power over their victims.

The role of escalation is further amplified by the killer's growing sense of invincibility. With each successful crime, they gain confidence in their ability to evade detection, leading them to take greater risks. They may begin leaving clues or taunting law enforcement, believing themselves untouchable. This arrogance can result in more public or sensational crimes, as they seek recognition or validation of their perceived superiority. However, this overconfidence often becomes their downfall, as the increased risk-taking provides investigators with more opportunities to catch them.

Escalation is not always linear; it can vary based on external factors, such as media attention, law enforcement pressure, or personal circumstances. Some killers may lie dormant for periods, suppressing their urges due to fear of capture or changes in their environment. However, this suppression often leads to a build-up of tension, resulting in an explosive return to violence that is even more intense than before. These cycles of inactivity and heightened activity are a hallmark of many serial killers and reflect the interplay between external constraints and internal compulsions.

The role of escalation also underscores the addictive nature of serial killing. For many killers, their crimes provide a psychological release or emotional high that they cannot achieve through other means. Like an addict chasing their next fix, they find that the same actions that once satisfied them are no longer enough. This need to escalate—to kill more frequently, violently, or elaborately—becomes a central driving force in their behavior. Each crime is not only an act of violence but also an attempt to satiate an ever-growing psychological hunger.

Ultimately, escalation is a window into the evolving psyche of serial killers. It reveals their growing confidence, their deepening compulsions, and their relentless pursuit of satisfaction through increasingly extreme acts. Understanding this process is critical for investigators, as it helps predict future behavior, identify patterns, and anticipate the killer's next moves. Escalation is not just a progression of actions; it is a reflection of the psychological unraveling that defines the predatory mind, where each crime builds upon the last in a chilling cycle of violence and obsession.

## How killers' methods evolve over time

The methods of serial killers often evolve over time, reflecting a combination of learning, adaptation, and deepening psychological needs. This evolution is a key characteristic of serial killers, as they continuously refine their techniques to become more efficient, evade detection, and achieve greater psychological satisfaction from their crimes. Understanding how these methods change offers critical insight into their mindset, motivations, and behavioral patterns.

In the early stages, a serial killer's methods are often experimental. Their first crime is typically unpolished, marked by hesitation, mistakes, or inefficiencies. This initial act serves as a trial run, where the killer tests their ability to carry out their fantasies in the real world. The aftermath of this first crime often provides a combination of exhilaration and dissatisfaction, as the killer reflects on what went right and what went wrong. This self-assessment becomes the foundation for refining their methods in subsequent acts.

As killers gain experience, their methods grow more sophisticated. They learn from their mistakes, becoming more adept at controlling their victims, avoiding evidence, and executing their plans with precision. For example, they may start using tools or techniques that minimize physical evidence, such as wearing gloves, choosing remote locations, or disposing of bodies in ways that delay discovery. These refinements are not only practical but also reflect the killer's growing confidence in their ability to operate undetected. The evolution of their methods often mirrors their increasing sense of mastery over their crimes.

Another factor driving the evolution of a killer's methods is their psychological need for escalation. Over time, the act of killing in its original form may no longer provide the same level of satisfaction. To recapture the emotional or psychological high, the killer may alter their methods to make the act more thrilling or fulfilling. This could involve increasing the level of violence, incorporating rituals, or selecting victims who fit a more specific profile. The changes in method are often tied to the killer's internal fantasies, which become more elaborate and demanding as they continue their spree.

The evolution of methods also reflects the killer's adaptability to external factors. Serial killers often adjust their techniques in response to law enforcement pressure or media attention. If a particular method draws too much attention or becomes predictable, they may change their approach to throw off investigators. For example, they might shift their hunting grounds, use different weapons, or alter the timing of their crimes. This adaptability is a survival mechanism, enabling them to continue their crimes while minimizing the risk of capture. However, these changes can also leave patterns that skilled investigators use to link crimes and profile the offender.

In some cases, killers develop a signature element in their methods, which remains consistent even as other aspects of their approach evolve. A signature reflects a personal or psychological need, such as taking a specific trophy or performing a particular act with the victim. While the logistics of their crimes may change, the signature often persists, providing investigators with valuable clues about the killer's identity and motivations. This tension between the evolving method and the fixed signature highlights the dual nature of serial killers as both pragmatic and deeply compulsive.

Killers' methods can also regress or become more chaotic as their psychological state deteriorates. Over time, the pressure of maintaining a double life, combined with the growing intensity of their compulsions, can lead to sloppier execution. This regression often results in a breakdown of their careful planning, leaving behind more evidence or exposing them to greater risks. Paradoxically, this decline in methodical behavior can accelerate their capture, as the errors they make provide law enforcement with new opportunities to apprehend them.

Ultimately, the evolution of a serial killer's methods is a reflection of their inner journey. It reveals their capacity to learn and adapt, their need for control and fulfillment, and their ability to balance pragmatism with psychological compulsion. By studying how these methods change over time, investigators can gain a deeper understanding of the killer's mindset, anticipate their next moves, and uncover the patterns that will eventually lead to their capture. The progression of their methods is not just a series of technical adjustments—it is a window into the escalating darkness of their predatory nature.

# Chapter 7: Twisted Motives

## Why Serial Killers Kill

Serial killers are driven by a variety of motives that reflect their internal desires, psychological needs, and distorted worldviews. Unlike crimes of passion or financial gain, the motives of serial killers are often deeply personal and psychological, rooted in fantasies that they seek to bring to life through their acts of violence. These motives can be broadly categorized into typologies such as power, control, lust, revenge, and thrill-seeking, though many killers display a complex interplay of these elements. Understanding these motivational typologies provides insight into the twisted logic that fuels their actions and offers a framework for profiling their behavior.

The desire for power and control is one of the most common motives among serial killers. These individuals crave dominance over others, often stemming from feelings of powerlessness or inadequacy in their own lives. By committing murder, they assert complete authority over their victims, choosing how and when they die. This motive is not limited to physical control but extends to psychological domination, as killers manipulate, terrify, and dehumanize their victims. Power-driven killers often target individuals they perceive as vulnerable or easy to overpower, reinforcing their sense of superiority and mastery.

Lust is another powerful motivator, particularly among killers who derive sexual gratification from their crimes. For these individuals, violence and sexuality are deeply intertwined, and the act of murder becomes a means of fulfilling their deviant fantasies. Lust-driven killers often select victims based on physical appearance or other traits that align with their desires, and their crimes frequently involve sexual assault or post-mortem violations. The pleasure they derive from these acts is not solely physical but also psychological, as they merge their fantasies with reality in a way that provides intense satisfaction. This category includes some of the most infamous and disturbing serial killers, whose actions are often marked by a ritualistic focus on their victims' bodies.

Revenge is another motive that drives some serial killers, particularly those who have experienced significant trauma, rejection, or abuse in their past. These individuals externalize their anger and pain, directing it toward victims who symbolize their grievances. For example, a killer who suffered abuse from a parental figure might target individuals who resemble or remind them of that person. Revenge-driven killers often justify their actions as a form of retribution, convincing themselves that their victims deserve to suffer. This motive is deeply personal and rooted in unresolved emotional wounds, making their crimes an extension of their internal struggles.

Thrill-seeking is a motive that reflects the killer's need for excitement, adrenaline, or the sheer pleasure of committing acts of violence. These killers are often driven by the thrill of the hunt, the act of overpowering their victims, and the danger involved in evading capture. For them, the act of killing is less about the victim and more about the experience itself. Thrill-seeking killers often escalate their crimes, seeking greater risks or more elaborate methods to sustain their psychological high. This motive highlights the addictive nature of their behavior, as each act of violence serves as both a release and a compulsion to repeat the experience.

Many serial killers are motivated by a combination of these typologies, rather than a single driving factor. For example, a killer might seek power and control while also experiencing sexual gratification from their crimes, or they might rationalize their actions as revenge while simultaneously seeking the thrill of the act. This interplay of motives makes their behavior highly complex and difficult to predict, as their actions are influenced by a range of psychological and emotional factors. Moreover, their motives can evolve over time, shifting as they gain confidence, refine their methods, or respond to external pressures.

These motivational typologies are not just abstract categories but are deeply rooted in the killers' psychological makeup and personal histories. They reflect the unresolved traumas, fantasies, and emotional voids that drive their actions, offering a glimpse into the dark and twisted logic that defines their behavior. By understanding these motives, investigators and psychologists can better analyze their patterns, anticipate their actions, and ultimately bring them to justice. Serial killers' motives are not merely the reason they kill—they are the foundation of their identity, the lens through which they view the world, and the driving force behind their descent into violence.

## Case studies of killers driven by different motives

Case studies of serial killers reveal how their motives—ranging from power and control to lust, revenge, and thrill-seeking—shape their actions and define their crimes. Each case provides a unique lens into the psychological drivers that compel these individuals to commit repeated acts of violence, highlighting the diversity of motives within the category of serial killers.

Ted Bundy is a quintessential example of a killer motivated by lust and power. Bundy's victims were predominantly young women who resembled his ex-girlfriend, which suggests that rejection and unresolved emotional pain played a role in shaping his crimes. Bundy lured his victims by exploiting their empathy, often pretending to have a physical injury, and once in control, he subjected them to brutal acts of violence, including sexual assault and post-mortem violations. His crimes reveal a deep connection between violence and sexual gratification, driven by fantasies of dominance. Bundy's ability to charm and manipulate people not only helped him evade capture for years but also underscored his need for control, extending even to his trial, where he acted as his own attorney to maintain power over the proceedings.

Aileen Wuornos represents a case of revenge-driven killings. A sex worker who killed seven men in Florida, Wuornos claimed that her victims had attempted to assault her, framing her actions as self-defense. However, her background of abuse, neglect, and exploitation points to a deeper motive of retaliating against men who symbolized the oppression she had endured throughout her life. Wuornos's crimes were not meticulously planned, and her impulsive actions highlight the emotional nature of her motive. Her case sheds light on how unresolved trauma and anger can drive serial violence, especially when combined with a life of social marginalization and instability.

Jeffrey Dahmer exemplifies a killer driven by lust and control, but with a uniquely disturbing twist. Dahmer targeted young men and boys, luring them to his home with promises of money or companionship. His crimes involved sexual assault, murder, and necrophilia, but what set Dahmer apart was his compulsion to exert ultimate control over his victims. He attempted to create compliant, zombie-like companions by performing crude brain surgeries on some victims, a chilling manifestation of his desire for total domination. Dahmer's actions reveal how fantasies of control and intimacy can spiral into grotesque extremes, highlighting the complex interplay between loneliness, rejection, and psychological compulsion.

John Wayne Gacy is a case study in power and control, with a layer of deception that added to his infamy. Gacy presented himself as a respectable member of the community, even dressing as a clown for children's events, while secretly luring young men and boys to their deaths. His victims were often coerced into restraints under the guise of a magic trick before being sexually assaulted and murdered. Gacy's crimes were meticulously planned, and his ability to maintain a double life reflects his need to dominate not only his victims but also the perception of those around him. Gacy's case demonstrates how killers can use trust and charm as tools to fulfill their dark desires for power and control.

Dennis Rader, known as the BTK Killer, offers a chilling example of a thrill-seeking killer with a need for recognition. Rader's acronym, "Bind, Torture, Kill," succinctly captured his methods, which he carried out with methodical precision. His crimes spanned decades, and he often taunted law enforcement with letters that detailed his actions, feeding his desire for attention and validation. For Rader, the thrill of the hunt and the satisfaction of evading capture were as important as the crimes themselves. His need to be acknowledged and feared added a layer of arrogance to his actions, ultimately leading to his capture when he resumed communication with authorities after years of silence.

Ed Kemper, known as the Co-Ed Killer, is an example of a killer driven by revenge and control. Kemper's crimes stemmed from deep-seated resentment toward his mother, whom he viewed as abusive and controlling. His early murders involved hitchhikers, but they culminated in the killing of his mother, whose body he mutilated in an act of symbolic revenge. Kemper's high intelligence and willingness to discuss his crimes openly after his capture have provided investigators with valuable insights into the psychological underpinnings of serial killers. His case illustrates how unresolved familial conflict and a need for dominance can drive violent behavior.

Richard Ramirez, the Night Stalker, exemplifies a thrill-seeking killer whose motives were rooted in chaos and destruction. Ramirez targeted a wide range of victims, from children to elderly individuals, using varied methods that included stabbing, shooting, and bludgeoning. His lack of a consistent victim profile or method added an element of unpredictability to his crimes, which were marked by the thrill he derived from spreading fear. Ramirez's fascination with Satanism and his taunts to law enforcement reflected his desire to create a legacy of terror, showing how thrill-seeking killers often crave notoriety alongside the adrenaline rush of their crimes.

These case studies highlight the diverse and deeply personal motives that drive serial killers. While their methods and behaviors may vary, their actions are unified by the twisted logic that compels them to kill repeatedly. Each case provides a unique perspective on the dark complexities of human psychology, offering insights that are as disturbing as they are vital to understanding and preventing such crimes.

# The psychological satisfaction derived from killing

The psychological satisfaction derived from killing is one of the most disturbing aspects of serial killers' behavior. Unlike crimes driven by financial gain or momentary rage, serial murders are often rooted in deep psychological gratification that motivates the killer to repeat their actions. For these individuals, the act of killing fulfills intense emotional, psychological, or even physical needs, making it an addictive and consuming compulsion. This satisfaction often stems from a combination of power, control, dominance, and the fulfillment of fantasies.

One of the primary sources of psychological satisfaction for serial killers is the sense of power and control over their victims. Many killers experience feelings of powerlessness or inadequacy in their personal lives, whether due to childhood trauma, rejection, or a lack of meaningful relationships. By taking the life of another person, they assert complete dominance, reducing their victims to objects under their control. This ability to dictate the fate of another human being provides a temporary sense of empowerment that compensates for their perceived weaknesses or failures. The act of overpowering their victims becomes a way for them to reclaim control in a world where they often feel powerless.

For some, the satisfaction comes from fulfilling long-held fantasies. Many serial killers develop elaborate mental scenarios in which they act out their desires, and the act of killing is the culmination of those fantasies. The victim often plays a specific role in these imagined narratives, and the killer's actions are meticulously designed to match the script in their mind. When these fantasies are realized, the killer experiences a sense of completion and gratification that reinforces their compulsion to kill again. However, this satisfaction is often fleeting, leading to a cycle in which they must commit another murder to recapture the same psychological high.

The emotional release provided by killing is another significant factor. Serial killers frequently harbor deep-seated anger, frustration, or resentment, often stemming from unresolved trauma or feelings of rejection. The act of killing serves as an outlet for these emotions, allowing them to release their internal tension through violence. This cathartic effect can create a sense of relief or satisfaction, as the killer feels momentarily unburdened by the emotional weight they carry. Over time, this need for release becomes a driving force, with each murder offering a temporary escape from their inner turmoil.

In cases involving sexual motivation, the act of killing is often intertwined with lust or arousal, providing a twisted form of physical gratification. For these killers, the violence itself is eroticized, and the murder becomes an extension of their deviant fantasies. The act of exerting total control over another person, often coupled with sexual assault or post-mortem acts, fulfills a psychological need that goes beyond physical pleasure. This combination of violence and sexual satisfaction creates an addictive feedback loop, where the killer becomes increasingly driven to reenact their fantasies to achieve the same level of gratification.

The psychological satisfaction derived from killing is also tied to the thrill of the act itself. For many serial killers, the process of stalking, capturing, and killing their victims provides an adrenaline rush akin to a high-stakes game. The danger of being caught, the careful planning required, and the execution of their crimes all contribute to a sense of excitement and exhilaration. This thrill-seeking behavior is often compared to an addiction, as the killer seeks increasingly daring or elaborate crimes to maintain the same level of stimulation.

Some serial killers derive satisfaction from the attention and fear their actions generate. By committing high-profile or sensational murders, they achieve a sense of notoriety that feeds their ego and validates their sense of superiority. This need for recognition is particularly evident in killers who taunt law enforcement or leave behind clues at crime scenes. For them, the act of killing is not just about the victim but also about the psychological satisfaction of being feared, admired, or even envied for their ability to outsmart those pursuing them.

Ultimately, the psychological satisfaction derived from killing is complex and multifaceted, reflecting the deep psychological dysfunctions and emotional voids of serial killers. For these individuals, murder is not just an act of violence but a means of achieving control, fulfilling fantasies, releasing pent-up emotions, or seeking validation. This satisfaction, however fleeting, reinforces their compulsion to kill, creating a dangerous cycle that continues until they are caught. Understanding this twisted sense of gratification is key to unraveling the motives and behaviors of serial killers, providing insights into the darkest corners of the human psyche.

# Chapter 8: Inside Infamous Minds

## Profiles of Notorious Serial Killers

The minds of serial killers offer a haunting glimpse into the extreme ends of human behavior, where psychological dysfunction, trauma, and deviance converge. Examining the profiles of notorious serial killers like Ted Bundy, Jeffrey Dahmer, Aileen Wuornos, and others reveals distinct patterns of behavior and motive while highlighting the complexities of their personalities and crimes. Each of these individuals presents a unique case, shaped by a combination of personal history, psychological disorders, and their need to fulfill twisted fantasies.

Ted Bundy is often regarded as the quintessential serial killer due to his charm, intelligence, and ability to manipulate those around him. Bundy's victims were predominantly young women who resembled his ex-girlfriend, pointing to a deep-seated need to reenact his personal rejection and regain power over figures he associated with pain or humiliation. Bundy lured his victims by feigning vulnerability, such as pretending to have a broken arm, before overpowering them and subjecting them to brutal sexual violence and murder. His crimes were methodical, and he displayed an unsettling ability to compartmentalize his predatory nature from his public persona. Bundy's narcissism and psychopathy were evident not only in his crimes but also in his behavior during his trial, where he represented himself in court, relishing the attention and control he commanded.

Jeffrey Dahmer, known as the Milwaukee Cannibal, represents a darker, more isolated type of killer. Dahmer's crimes were rooted in his desire for complete control and companionship. He targeted young men, luring them to his home with promises of money or photographs, where he drugged, murdered, and sometimes cannibalized them. Dahmer's actions extended beyond murder to include disturbing experiments, such as attempting to create "zombie-like" victims through crude brain surgeries. These acts reflected his deep fear of abandonment and his inability to form meaningful relationships. Dahmer's necrophilic tendencies and cannibalism further underscore his need to possess his victims completely, even after their deaths. Despite the horrific nature of his crimes, Dahmer displayed remorse after his capture, offering a rare glimpse into the conflict between his compulsions and his awareness of their wrongness.

Aileen Wuornos, often referred to as America's first female serial killer, presents a case rooted in trauma, survival, and revenge. Unlike many male serial killers, Wuornos's crimes were less calculated and more emotionally driven. As a sex worker, she targeted men who solicited her services, shooting them at point-blank range. Wuornos claimed her killings were in self-defense, alleging that her victims had attempted to harm or assault her. However, evidence suggested her actions were often premeditated, driven by deep-seated anger and resentment toward men. Wuornos's turbulent upbringing, marked by abuse, neglect, and abandonment, shaped her worldview and fueled her rage. Her case challenges traditional notions of serial killers, as her actions were deeply tied to her own victimization and survival instincts.

John Wayne Gacy, the "Killer Clown," offers a chilling example of a double life. Gacy was a respected member of his community, known for hosting parties and dressing as a clown to entertain children. However, beneath this façade lay a sadistic predator who lured young men and boys to his home, where he raped and murdered them. Gacy buried many of his victims in the crawl space of his house, a macabre detail that symbolized his need to conceal his crimes while maintaining control over the bodies. Gacy's ability to blend into society highlights the dangers of assuming that evil is easily recognizable. His crimes reflected his need for dominance, control, and a perverse sense of power over his victims.

Richard Ramirez, the "Night Stalker," terrorized California with a spree of home invasions, rapes, and murders. Ramirez's lack of a consistent victim profile, targeting men, women, and children of varying ages, added an unpredictable element to his crimes. His actions were driven by thrill-seeking, sadistic pleasure, and a fascination with Satanism, which he used to justify and ritualize his killings. Ramirez thrived on the chaos and fear he created, often leaving satanic symbols at his crime scenes to taunt law enforcement and heighten public terror. His case demonstrates how killers can use unpredictability as a weapon, making them more difficult to profile and capture.

Ed Kemper, the "Co-Ed Killer," offers one of the most chilling profiles of intelligence and brutality. Kemper began his criminal career by murdering his grandparents as a teenager, only to escalate his crimes after his release from a psychiatric facility. He targeted female college students, luring them into his car before killing them and dismembering their bodies. Kemper's deep resentment toward his abusive mother was a central theme in his killings, culminating in her murder and the desecration of her body. Despite the horrific nature of his crimes, Kemper displayed remarkable self-awareness and cooperated with investigators after his capture, providing insights into the psychology of serial killers.

These profiles reveal that serial killers are not a monolithic group but a diverse collection of individuals shaped by their unique circumstances, psychological disorders, and motivations. From the calculated charm of Ted Bundy to the emotional volatility of Aileen Wuornos, each killer represents a different facet of the human psyche turned dark. Studying their lives and crimes provides critical insights into the patterns and motivations of serial killers, helping law enforcement and psychologists better understand, anticipate, and prevent these acts of violence. At the same time, these cases serve as a sobering reminder of the extremes of human behavior and the complexity of the forces that drive individuals to kill.

## Their psychological profiles and unique patterns of predation

The psychological profiles of serial killers and their unique patterns of predation reveal the intricate and disturbing ways their minds operate. These profiles are shaped by a combination of deep-seated psychological disorders, unresolved trauma, and the compulsion to fulfill deviant fantasies. While no two killers are exactly alike, they often share certain traits, such as a lack of empathy, a need for control, and an ability to mask their true intentions behind a facade of normalcy. Their patterns of predation, however, are as unique as their motivations, shaped by their psychological makeup, personal experiences, and the fantasies that drive their actions.

A defining characteristic of many serial killers is their ability to compartmentalize their lives, allowing them to maintain a seemingly normal existence while secretly engaging in acts of violence. This duality is a hallmark of psychopathy, a disorder commonly associated with serial killers. Psychopaths are highly manipulative, emotionally detached, and skilled at presenting themselves as trustworthy and even charming. This allows them to blend into society, evade suspicion, and gain access to potential victims. Their ability to feign normalcy is often a critical element of their predatory strategy, as it enables them to lure victims without raising alarm.

The need for power and control is another central aspect of their psychological profiles. Many serial killers come from backgrounds marked by abuse, neglect, or rejection, which leave them feeling powerless and inadequate. Killing becomes a way to assert dominance and regain a sense of control over their lives. This need for control often extends to their methods of predation. Serial killers meticulously plan their crimes, selecting victims who fit specific criteria and crafting scenarios that allow them to manipulate their targets. This calculated approach reflects their desire to exert complete authority over their victims, both physically and psychologically.

Their patterns of predation are closely tied to their fantasies, which often serve as blueprints for their actions. These fantasies are deeply personal and vary widely among killers. Some focus on the physical characteristics of their victims, targeting individuals who resemble a specific figure from their past, such as an abusive parent or an ex-lover. Others are drawn to symbolic elements, such as age, occupation, or lifestyle, that align with their imagined narratives. These preferences shape not only who they target but also how they approach and interact with their victims, making their patterns of predation a direct reflection of their inner worlds.

Geographic behavior also plays a significant role in their predation patterns. Many serial killers operate within a defined comfort zone, targeting victims in areas they know well. This familiarity provides a sense of security, reducing the risk of detection and allowing them to observe potential targets over time. Others, particularly those with a nomadic lifestyle or access to transportation, may extend their hunting grounds over larger areas, making their crimes harder to connect. This variation in geographic behavior is often influenced by the killer's personality, level of organization, and need for control.

The evolution of their predation patterns over time is another important element of their psychological profiles. Early in their careers, serial killers may act impulsively or sloppily, learning from their mistakes and refining their methods as they gain experience. This progression reflects their growing confidence and mastery over their crimes. However, their methods can also become more erratic or escalatory, driven by a need for greater thrills or by external pressures, such as law enforcement attention. These changes in behavior provide valuable clues to investigators, as they reveal the killer's psychological state and potential vulnerabilities.

Their lack of empathy and emotional detachment also define their approach to predation. Serial killers often view their victims as objects rather than individuals, reducing them to tools for fulfilling their desires. This dehumanization allows them to commit acts of violence without remorse or guilt. For some, this detachment is evident in their post-mortem actions, such as mutilation or trophy-taking, which serve to reinforce their fantasies and prolong the psychological gratification of the kill. These behaviors further highlight their inability to form meaningful emotional connections, a common trait in their psychological profiles.

In understanding the psychological profiles and patterns of predation of serial killers, it becomes clear that their actions are not random but deeply rooted in their psyche. Their behaviors are shaped by a combination of psychological disorders, personal history, and a compulsion to bring their fantasies to life. These patterns offer critical insights into their motivations and methods, helping law enforcement and psychologists anticipate their actions and work toward prevention. The study of their predatory behavior is not only essential for solving crimes but also for understanding the extreme and unsettling capacities of the human mind.

## Lessons learned from their crimes

The crimes of serial killers, while horrifying, offer valuable lessons that extend beyond the violence itself, providing insights into human behavior, law enforcement strategies, societal vulnerabilities, and the importance of early intervention. These lessons are critical not only for understanding how to apprehend and prevent such individuals from acting but also for addressing the underlying conditions that may contribute to the emergence of serial offenders.

One of the most significant lessons learned from the crimes of serial killers is the importance of early identification and intervention. Many killers exhibit troubling behaviors during childhood or adolescence, such as cruelty to animals, fire-setting, or chronic antisocial tendencies, which are often dismissed as mere behavioral issues. Addressing these warning signs with psychological support, therapy, or other interventions can potentially disrupt the development of violent tendencies. By recognizing and acting on these red flags, families, educators, and mental health professionals can play a vital role in preventing future violence.

The study of serial killers has also highlighted the critical role of psychological profiling and behavioral analysis in law enforcement. Over the years, investigators have developed sophisticated profiling techniques that use patterns in a killer's behavior, victim selection, and crime scene evidence to build psychological and demographic profiles. These tools have proven invaluable in narrowing suspect pools and predicting future actions. High-profile cases like those of Ted Bundy and Dennis Rader (the BTK Killer) have demonstrated the effectiveness of these methods, leading to their refinement and integration into modern investigative practices.

Another lesson learned is the need for inter-agency collaboration and data sharing in solving serial crimes. Many serial killers operate across multiple jurisdictions, exploiting gaps in communication between law enforcement agencies. The creation of centralized systems like the FBI's Violent Criminal Apprehension Program (ViCAP) was born from the recognition that linking crimes through shared data is essential in identifying patterns and catching offenders. Cases such as those of John Wayne Gacy and Gary Ridgway (the Green River Killer) revealed the challenges of fragmented investigations and underscored the importance of coordinated efforts.

The crimes of serial killers also shed light on societal vulnerabilities that can make certain individuals more likely to become victims. Many killers target individuals who are marginalized, such as sex workers, runaways, or those living in poverty, knowing that their disappearances may attract less attention. These patterns reveal a need for greater societal protections for vulnerable populations and stronger community support systems to prevent individuals from becoming easy targets for predators. Raising awareness and providing resources to these groups can reduce their susceptibility to exploitation and violence.

Another key lesson is the importance of public awareness and education in identifying and preventing serial crime. Many killers maintain a facade of normalcy, often living undetected within their communities for years. Encouraging individuals to trust their instincts and report suspicious behavior can play a critical role in early detection. For example, tips from the public were instrumental in the capture of Richard Ramirez (the Night Stalker) and other high-profile offenders. Empowering communities with knowledge about warning signs and encouraging vigilance can create a more proactive approach to crime prevention.

Serial killers also teach us about the complexities of human psychology and the capacity for darkness within the human mind. Their crimes force us to confront uncomfortable truths about the interplay between nature and nurture, the impact of trauma, and the consequences of unaddressed mental health issues. These lessons emphasize the importance of mental health support at all levels of society, from early childhood interventions to accessible care for adults experiencing emotional or psychological struggles.

From a law enforcement perspective, the study of serial killers has underscored the importance of patience, persistence, and adaptability in investigations. Many cases take years or even decades to solve, requiring investigators to navigate dead ends, false leads, and evolving methodologies. Advances in forensic science, such as DNA analysis, have revolutionized the ability to solve cold cases, demonstrating the importance of continually integrating new technologies into investigative practices. The resolution of long-unsolved cases, such as those involving the Golden State Killer, highlights how perseverance and innovation can eventually bring justice to victims and their families.

Finally, the crimes of serial killers highlight the importance of prioritizing the victims and their families in the aftermath of violence. Too often, the focus shifts to the killer's psychology or notoriety, overshadowing the human cost of their actions. Ensuring that victims are remembered, their stories are told, and their families receive support is essential for fostering healing and maintaining the dignity of those affected by such tragedies.

In studying the lessons learned from serial killers, we gain not only the tools to prevent and solve such crimes but also a deeper understanding of the societal, psychological, and systemic factors that allow these individuals to operate. While their actions represent the darkest corners of human behavior, the knowledge gained from their crimes can illuminate paths toward prevention, intervention, and justice.

# Chapter 9: The Role of Society

## Cultural and Historical Influences

Societal norms and values play a significant role in shaping the behaviors and motivations of serial killers. While the psychological and personal factors driving these individuals are well-documented, the cultural and historical context in which they operate profoundly influences their actions, choices of victims, and the ways in which their crimes unfold. Society acts as both a mirror and a mold, reflecting the values of the time while simultaneously providing the conditions that enable serial killers to thrive.

One of the most striking ways societal norms influence serial killers is through the selection of their victims. Many killers target individuals who align with their internal fantasies, but those fantasies are often shaped by societal expectations and cultural archetypes. For example, the prominence of patriarchal values in many societies has historically led to the objectification and devaluation of women, making them common targets for male serial killers. Ted Bundy, for instance, targeted women who conformed to a particular ideal of attractiveness, reflecting societal standards of beauty and gender roles. Similarly, killers like Jack the Ripper preyed on sex workers, taking advantage of the societal stigma surrounding these women, which often resulted in less public and law enforcement attention when they went missing.

Cultural values also shape the methods and motivations of serial killers. In societies that glorify power, dominance, and control, some killers may internalize these ideals and act out violently to assert their own sense of superiority. For example, John Wayne Gacy's dual life as a respected community member and a sadistic murderer highlighted the societal pressures to maintain appearances while secretly indulging in deviant behaviors. Conversely, in cultures that emphasize individualism and self-promotion, killers may seek notoriety, viewing their crimes as a way to gain recognition or leave a legacy. Richard Ramirez, the Night Stalker, exemplified this, reveling in the public fear and media attention generated by his crimes.

The media, as a product of societal norms, also plays a significant role in influencing serial killer behavior. The sensationalized coverage of high-profile cases often elevates killers to celebrity status, inadvertently glamorizing their actions. Killers like Dennis Rader (BTK) and David Berkowitz (Son of Sam) thrived on the media attention they received, using it to fuel their egos and taunt law enforcement. In some cases, the media's portrayal of serial killers as enigmatic masterminds or anti-heroes can inspire copycat crimes, perpetuating a cycle of violence that feeds off societal fascination with the macabre.

Historical events and societal upheavals also influence the emergence and behavior of serial killers. Periods of war, economic instability, and social change often create conditions of chaos and vulnerability, providing opportunities for predators to exploit. For example, the post-World War II era saw a surge in serial killings in the United States, coinciding with rapid urbanization, shifting gender roles, and the rise of media culture. These changes created a fertile ground for killers to operate, as traditional community structures eroded and public fear increased. In contrast, tightly controlled or authoritarian societies may suppress the visibility of serial killers, as state-controlled media and law enforcement prioritize maintaining order over transparency.

Societal attitudes toward mental health and criminal justice also play a critical role in shaping serial killer behaviors. In societies where mental health issues are stigmatized or ignored, individuals who display early warning signs of violence may not receive the intervention they need. This neglect allows their destructive tendencies to grow unchecked. Additionally, law enforcement practices and resources reflect societal priorities. In cases where victims come from marginalized or vulnerable populations, such as sex workers or homeless individuals, investigations may be deprioritized, giving serial killers the opportunity to continue their crimes with minimal risk of capture. This was evident in the case of Gary Ridgway, the Green River Killer, whose targeting of sex workers delayed a comprehensive investigation into his crimes.

Cultural narratives about violence and justice also shape how serial killers justify their actions. In societies where vengeance or retribution is glorified, some killers may frame their murders as a form of personal justice or moral correction. Aileen Wuornos, for example, claimed to have killed in self-defense against abusive men, reflecting societal conversations about gender dynamics and victimhood. These justifications are often a twisted reflection of cultural values, distorted by the killer's own psychological needs and experiences.

Finally, societal fascination with serial killers plays a paradoxical role in both deterring and encouraging their behavior. While public awareness and education about serial crimes can lead to better prevention and detection, the cultural obsession with true crime stories, documentaries, and fictional portrayals often creates an allure that some killers find irresistible. The desire to become a part of this narrative or achieve infamy can motivate individuals to act, transforming their crimes into performances designed to capture public attention.

In understanding the role of society, it becomes clear that serial killers are not created in isolation. Their behaviors are shaped by the cultural and historical context in which they live, reflecting the values, norms, and contradictions of their time. By examining these societal influences, we gain not only a deeper understanding of the killers themselves but also the ways in which our own culture and institutions can enable or prevent such acts of violence. Addressing these broader systemic factors is essential for creating a society that is less vulnerable to the emergence of serial predators.

## The link between societal upheaval and the rise of serial killer

The link between societal upheaval and the rise of serial killers lies in the conditions of instability, fear, and disconnection that such upheavals create. Periods of significant social, economic, or political disruption often result in a breakdown of traditional structures and norms, leaving communities vulnerable to exploitation by predatory individuals. Serial killers thrive in these environments, where chaos and uncertainty provide opportunities for them to act undetected while amplifying the psychological and cultural factors that drive their behavior.

Societal upheavals often lead to increased social isolation, a factor that serial killers exploit to target victims more easily. Economic downturns, rapid urbanization, or migration disrupt tight-knit communities, replacing them with anonymous environments where people are less connected to one another. In such settings, individuals on the margins of society, such as sex workers, runaways, or the homeless, become even more vulnerable, as their disappearances are less likely to be noticed or reported. This anonymity gives serial killers the freedom to operate with reduced risk of detection, as was evident in the cases of killers like Gary Ridgway, who targeted marginalized individuals during a time of social and economic shifts.

Periods of upheaval also weaken institutions, including law enforcement and the judicial system, creating gaps that serial killers can exploit. Wars, economic recessions, or political unrest often strain public resources, leading to underfunded or overwhelmed police forces. This was evident in post-World War II America, where a surge in violent crimes, including serial killings, coincided with rapid urbanization and shifting societal dynamics. In these conditions, serial killers were often able to act with impunity, taking advantage of fragmented investigations and lack of inter-agency collaboration. Jack the Ripper, operating in 19th-century London, is another example; his crimes occurred during a period of social inequality and police inefficiency, which contributed to his ability to evade capture.

Cultural changes during societal upheavals can also play a role in the rise of serial killers. Shifts in gender roles, technological advancements, and the emergence of mass media influence not only the behavior of killers but also how their crimes are perceived and investigated. For example, the feminist movement of the 1960s and 1970s brought increased independence for women, leading to more women entering public spaces, such as workplaces and universities. While this progress was a societal gain, it also created new opportunities for predatory individuals like Ted Bundy, who exploited these changing dynamics to target young women. Similarly, the rise of the automobile provided killers with greater mobility, allowing them to expand their hunting grounds and evade detection.

Societal upheaval often leads to a heightened cultural fascination with violence, which can indirectly fuel the rise of serial killers. During times of instability, people turn to media for explanations and narratives, leading to an increased focus on sensational crimes. This attention not only creates fear but also elevates the profile of serial killers, granting them the notoriety some seek. Killers like Richard Ramirez and Dennis Rader thrived on the public attention their crimes generated, using societal fear and media coverage to bolster their egos and continue their reigns of terror. In this way, societal disruption and the accompanying cultural fixation on violence can create a feedback loop, where the fear and fascination surrounding serial killers contribute to their persistence.

Psychologically, societal upheaval often exacerbates the underlying conditions that lead to the development of serial killers. Individuals who are predisposed to violent behavior, whether through genetic factors, trauma, or mental illness, may find their impulses amplified during periods of social instability. Economic struggles, displacement, and fractured families create environments where unresolved anger, resentment, and a need for control can fester. These emotions often fuel the fantasies and compulsions that drive serial killers, transforming personal grievances into acts of violence.

The aftermath of societal upheaval can also play a role in the rise of serial killers. Wars, for example, often leave a legacy of desensitization to violence, as well as populations struggling with trauma and displacement. Soldiers returning from combat or communities exposed to prolonged conflict may grapple with untreated psychological wounds, creating environments where violence becomes normalized or internalized. While not all individuals affected by war or social upheaval become violent offenders, the cultural and psychological shifts that follow these events can contribute to the conditions in which serial killers emerge.

The link between societal upheaval and the rise of serial killers ultimately underscores the interplay between individual pathology and external conditions. Serial killers are not created in isolation; their actions reflect both their internal drives and the environments in which they operate. By understanding how societal instability influences the emergence of these individuals, we can better address the systemic vulnerabilities that allow them to thrive, from improving community connections and law enforcement coordination to fostering resilience in the face of cultural and historical disruptions. Recognizing this connection is essential not only for preventing future violence but also for understanding the broader impact of societal change on human behavior.

## Comparing patterns across different cultures and eras

Serial killers, while often seen as products of individual pathology, are also influenced by the cultural and historical contexts in which they operate. Comparing patterns across different cultures and eras reveals significant variations in their methods, victim selection, and motivations, shaped by societal norms, technological advancements, and historical conditions. These differences provide a broader understanding of how serial killing transcends time and place while adapting to unique environmental and cultural influences.

In Western societies, particularly during the 20th century, serial killers like Ted Bundy and Jeffrey Dahmer often operated in urban or suburban environments, targeting victims who fit specific physical or social profiles. Their crimes were marked by calculated planning, the use of modern transportation, and a focus on individuals whose lifestyles or social positions rendered them vulnerable, such as hitchhikers or young men in marginalized communities. These patterns reflect the social and technological advancements of the time, including increased mobility and the loosening of traditional community structures, which provided opportunities for predators to exploit anonymity and transient lifestyles.

In contrast, serial killers in pre-industrial societies or less urbanized regions often displayed different patterns influenced by their environment. Historical cases, such as those of Gilles de Rais in 15th-century France or Elizabeth Báthory in 16th-century Hungary, reveal killers who targeted victims within their immediate vicinity, often using their positions of power to conceal their crimes. These individuals frequently preyed on peasants, servants, or those of lower social standing, reflecting the rigid class structures and limited oversight of their eras. The lack of centralized law enforcement and the isolation of rural communities provided these killers with the freedom to act over extended periods without detection.

Cultural attitudes toward gender also significantly influence patterns of serial killing. In many Western cases, serial killers are predominantly male, and their crimes often reflect patriarchal norms that dehumanize women and position them as targets for violence. However, in some cultures, female serial killers emerge with distinct patterns, often using poison or other less physically aggressive methods to kill their victims.

Historical examples, such as the "Angel Makers" of Nagyrév in Hungary, a group of women who poisoned family members and spouses during the early 20th century, highlight how societal constraints on women's physical agency shape their methods and motives. In these cases, the killers' actions often reflect systemic oppression, such as forced marriages or economic dependency, creating conditions that fostered violence as a means of escape or retaliation.

Religious and spiritual beliefs also play a critical role in shaping serial killer patterns across cultures and eras. In some cases, killers use religious justifications for their actions, framing their murders as acts of divine will or moral correction. Jack the Ripper, for example, operated in Victorian England during a period of heightened anxiety about morality and social reform, with his crimes targeting sex workers in a way that echoed broader societal concerns about vice and degradation. Similarly, killers in non-Western societies, such as those operating under the guise of witchcraft or ritual sacrifice, often reflect deeply ingrained cultural beliefs about power, purity, or the supernatural. These crimes highlight how cultural narratives can be distorted by killers to rationalize or ritualize their actions.

The impact of media and technology on serial killer patterns also varies across cultures and eras. In societies with developed media industries, killers often gain notoriety through sensationalized coverage, which can influence their behavior and even inspire copycat crimes. Richard Ramirez and Dennis Rader are prime examples of killers who fed off media attention, using public fear to fuel their egos and prolong their crimes. In contrast, in societies with limited media infrastructure or during historical periods without mass communication, serial killings were less likely to gain widespread attention, allowing killers to operate in obscurity. This lack of visibility often meant that patterns were harder to identify and connect, leaving communities vulnerable to prolonged predation.

Economic conditions further influence serial killer patterns across cultures and eras. In times of economic hardship or social inequality, marginalized individuals are often disproportionately targeted. For example, the victims of the Yorkshire Ripper in 1970s England were largely sex workers, a reflection of both societal stigma and the economic vulnerability of these women. Similarly, in developing countries or regions experiencing political instability, serial killers may target displaced individuals, orphans, or refugees, exploiting the chaos and lack of accountability in such environments.

The availability of forensic and investigative tools also shapes serial killer patterns. In modern Western societies, advances in DNA technology, geographic profiling, and database systems have made it increasingly difficult for serial killers to evade detection. This has pushed some killers toward more remote or less regulated areas where such tools are less accessible. By contrast, in historical periods or in regions with limited forensic capabilities, killers could act with greater impunity, relying on the lack of scientific evidence and jurisdictional collaboration to avoid capture.

Despite these variations, certain patterns remain consistent across cultures and eras. Serial killers often exhibit a need for control, a lack of empathy, and an ability to manipulate their environments. Their crimes are typically rooted in personal gratification, whether it stems from power, revenge, lust, or thrill-seeking, and they exploit societal vulnerabilities, such as marginalized populations or gaps in law enforcement. By comparing these patterns, we can better understand not only the universal aspects of serial killing but also the ways in which cultural and historical contexts shape the manifestation of these crimes. This knowledge is essential for tailoring investigative approaches and preventative measures to the unique challenges posed by different societies and periods.

# Chapter 10: The Science of Detection

## Catching Serial Killers

The science of detecting serial killers has evolved significantly over the decades, driven by advancements in forensic psychology, behavioral profiling, and investigative techniques. Early efforts to catch these elusive predators were often hindered by a lack of understanding about their behavior and motivations. However, the development of modern profiling methods and forensic tools has revolutionized the process, providing law enforcement with critical insights into the minds of serial killers and helping to connect seemingly unrelated crimes.

Forensic psychology, which focuses on understanding criminal behavior through psychological principles, has become a cornerstone in the investigation of serial killings. This field emerged in the mid-20th century, with psychologists and criminologists beginning to explore the motivations, thought patterns, and emotional triggers of violent offenders. Early pioneers, such as Dr. James Brussel, demonstrated the potential of psychological analysis when he profiled the "Mad Bomber" in the 1950s, predicting details about the perpetrator that proved eerily accurate. These early successes laid the groundwork for applying psychology to serial crimes, where the unique and repetitive nature of the offenses made behavioral analysis particularly useful.

Behavioral profiling, often synonymous with the FBI's Behavioral Analysis Unit (BAU), represents a more specialized application of forensic psychology. Profiling involves analyzing crime scene evidence, victimology, and offender behavior to create a psychological and demographic portrait of the killer.

This method gained prominence in the 1970s and 1980s, with agents like John Douglas and Robert Ressler at the forefront of its development. Their work, chronicled in books like Mindhunter, introduced the concept of categorizing killers as organized or disorganized, based on their crime scenes and methods. Organized killers are methodical, plan their crimes, and often leave little evidence, reflecting higher intelligence and control. Disorganized killers, on the other hand, act impulsively, leaving chaotic crime scenes that reflect their emotional instability. This distinction provides investigators with critical clues about the offender's personality and lifestyle.

The evolution of behavioral profiling also led to the development of offender typologies. Profilers began identifying patterns in the motives and methods of serial killers, categorizing them as power-driven, lust-driven, revenge-driven, or thrill-seeking. These classifications help narrow suspect pools and predict future actions by understanding the psychological needs driving the killer. For example, power-driven killers like Dennis Rader (BTK) leave clues to taunt law enforcement, while lust-driven killers like Jeffrey Dahmer focus on fulfilling deviant sexual fantasies. By studying these patterns, profilers can anticipate how and where the killer might strike next.

Advancements in forensic science have further enhanced the ability to detect and apprehend serial killers. The introduction of DNA analysis in the 1980s was a game-changer, allowing investigators to link crimes through genetic evidence. Cases like the capture of the Golden State Killer, who was identified decades after his crimes through familial DNA, demonstrate the power of this technology. Fingerprinting, blood spatter analysis, and fiber evidence have also played crucial roles in connecting crime scenes and identifying suspects. These forensic tools provide the hard evidence needed to complement the psychological insights gained from profiling.

Geographic profiling, another major innovation, focuses on the spatial patterns of a killer's crimes to identify their likely base of operations. This method is based on the principle of distance decay, which suggests that offenders are more likely to commit crimes closer to their home or a familiar area. By mapping crime scenes and analyzing the distances between them, investigators can predict where the killer might live or operate. Geographic profiling was instrumental in solving cases like those of the Green River Killer, where a clear pattern of victim locations helped narrow the search area.

Collaboration between law enforcement agencies has also been critical in the evolution of serial killer detection. Killers often exploit jurisdictional boundaries, committing crimes in different areas to avoid detection. The creation of centralized databases, such as the FBI's Violent Criminal Apprehension Program (ViCAP), allows investigators to share information and identify patterns across state or national borders. This level of cooperation has been pivotal in linking crimes that might otherwise have been treated as isolated incidents.

The role of technology in modern investigations cannot be overstated. Advances in surveillance systems, data analytics, and digital forensics have made it increasingly difficult for killers to evade capture. Tools like license plate recognition, cellphone tracking, and online activity monitoring provide investigators with new ways to trace offenders. For example, many modern killers have been apprehended through their digital footprints, such as online searches or social media activity. These tools not only help in solving active cases but also in revisiting cold cases, offering hope to victims' families decades after crimes were committed.

Despite these advancements, catching serial killers remains a complex and challenging task. While forensic psychology and profiling provide valuable insights, they are not infallible. The science of detection requires a combination of psychological expertise, technological innovation, and traditional investigative work. Each case brings its own set of challenges, requiring investigators to adapt their methods and think creatively to outsmart predators who are often intelligent, manipulative, and highly adaptable.

The evolution of forensic psychology and behavioral profiling has transformed the way serial killers are understood and pursued. By combining psychological analysis with cutting-edge technology and collaborative efforts, law enforcement has made significant strides in detecting and apprehending these criminals. However, the process continues to evolve as new technologies and methodologies emerge, ensuring that the science of detection remains a critical tool in the fight against the darkest aspects of human behavior.

## Advances in DNA technology and crime scene analysis

Advances in DNA technology and crime scene analysis have revolutionized the field of criminal investigation, providing law enforcement with powerful tools to identify perpetrators and link crimes with unprecedented accuracy. DNA evidence, first introduced in the 1980s, marked a turning point in forensic science by allowing investigators to extract and analyze genetic material left behind at crime scenes. Over the decades, these advancements have become more sophisticated, enabling the resolution of cold cases, the exoneration of wrongfully accused individuals, and the identification of serial offenders.

One of the most significant breakthroughs in DNA technology is the development of polymerase chain reaction (PCR) techniques. PCR allows even the smallest, degraded DNA samples to be amplified and analyzed, making it possible to extract usable genetic material from evidence that would have been considered unusable in the past. This has proven especially valuable in older cases, where DNA samples have deteriorated over time, and in crimes where only trace amounts of biological material, such as skin cells or a single hair follicle, are available.

Another transformative innovation is the use of short tandem repeats (STR) in DNA profiling. STR analysis examines specific regions of the DNA that vary greatly between individuals, providing a highly reliable means of identifying suspects or linking evidence to known profiles. This method is faster and more precise than earlier techniques, allowing for rapid comparison of DNA samples against national and international databases. Systems like the FBI's Combined DNA Index System (CODIS) have become invaluable in solving crimes, enabling law enforcement to match DNA from crime scenes to offenders in the database or link crimes committed by the same individual across different jurisdictions.

Familial DNA searches represent another groundbreaking advancement. This technique involves searching DNA databases for partial matches, identifying relatives of potential suspects when no direct match is found. Familial DNA analysis has been instrumental in solving high-profile cases, such as the apprehension of the Golden State Killer. By identifying a close relative through genealogical databases, investigators were able to narrow down the suspect pool and ultimately link the killer to crimes committed decades earlier. This approach has extended the reach of DNA technology, allowing cases to be solved even when the suspect's DNA is not in any database.

Touch DNA, or trace DNA analysis, has further expanded the scope of crime scene investigation. This method involves extracting DNA from microscopic amounts of biological material left behind when a person touches an object or surface. Touch DNA has been used to analyze evidence that traditional methods would have overlooked, such as weapons, clothing, or even surfaces like door handles. This innovation has allowed investigators to piece together events with greater detail, connecting suspects to crime scenes or objects they may have handled during the commission of a crime.

Advances in rapid DNA testing have also streamlined the investigative process. These portable systems can generate DNA profiles within hours, rather than the weeks or months required by traditional lab-based methods. Rapid DNA technology has proven particularly valuable in time-sensitive cases, such as identifying suspects in active investigations or confirming the identity of individuals at crime scenes. By providing near-instant results, this technology allows law enforcement to act more quickly, potentially preventing further crimes or securing critical evidence before it is compromised.

Crime scene analysis has also benefited from technological advancements beyond DNA. High-resolution imaging, 3D laser scanning, and digital reconstruction tools allow investigators to create detailed visual representations of crime scenes, preserving critical information long after the physical site has been cleared. These tools enable forensic experts to analyze evidence with greater precision, from mapping blood spatter patterns to understanding the sequence of events during a crime. Coupled with DNA evidence, these techniques provide a comprehensive picture of what occurred, helping to corroborate witness testimony or refute false alibis.

The integration of DNA technology with artificial intelligence and machine learning is another frontier in crime scene analysis. AI algorithms can process vast amounts of genetic data, identifying patterns and connections that might elude human investigators. These systems can also analyze mixed DNA samples, where genetic material from multiple individuals is present, disentangling complex evidence to provide clear, actionable insights. This capability has proven invaluable in cases involving mass casualties or crimes with multiple perpetrators.

The cumulative effect of these advancements is a dramatic increase in the ability to solve crimes and hold offenders accountable. DNA technology and modern crime scene analysis have shifted the balance in favor of law enforcement, making it increasingly difficult for criminals to evade capture. Cold cases that once seemed unsolvable are now being reopened and resolved, bringing long-awaited closure to victims and their families. At the same time, these tools have strengthened the fairness of the justice system by reducing the risk of wrongful convictions and ensuring that evidence is analyzed with the highest degree of accuracy.

As DNA technology and crime scene analysis continue to evolve, the future holds even greater potential for innovation. Emerging techniques like environmental DNA (eDNA), which can extract genetic material from the environment, and advancements in genome sequencing promise to further enhance forensic capabilities. These developments underscore the transformative power of science in solving crimes, illuminating the path toward a more effective and just criminal justice system.

### How police track patterns and link murders.

Police track patterns and link murders by using a combination of forensic evidence, behavioral analysis, technological tools, and data-sharing systems to identify connections between seemingly unrelated crimes. Serial murders, by their nature, are often committed in different locations and over extended periods, making it challenging to identify a single perpetrator without recognizing consistent patterns in behavior, methods, and victimology. Modern investigative techniques have evolved to address these challenges, allowing law enforcement to detect links and build comprehensive profiles of offenders.

One of the primary methods used to link murders is the analysis of crime scene evidence. Forensic science plays a critical role, with DNA testing, fingerprint analysis, and ballistic matching providing concrete connections between cases. For example, DNA recovered from multiple crime scenes can reveal a common perpetrator, even if the crimes occurred years apart. Ballistic analysis, which examines bullet striations and firearm markings, can link shootings to the same weapon, helping investigators identify patterns in cases involving firearms. Similarly, forensic analysis of fibers, blood spatter, or trace materials can establish connections between victims, crime scenes, or methods.

Behavioral patterns also provide critical clues in linking murders. Serial killers often display consistent methods of operation, known as their modus operandi (MO), which includes how they select victims, carry out the crime, and dispose of evidence. While MOs may evolve over time as killers adapt or learn from their mistakes, certain aspects often remain consistent enough to reveal a pattern. Beyond the MO, investigators also look for signatures—unique behaviors or ritualistic actions that are psychologically significant to the killer but unnecessary for committing the crime. These signatures, such as posing victims in specific ways or leaving symbolic items at the scene, are highly distinctive and help link murders to a single individual.

Victimology—the study of the victims—provides another avenue for identifying patterns. By analyzing the demographics, lifestyles, and behaviors of victims, investigators can uncover commonalities that point to a specific killer. For instance, a serial killer might target individuals of a particular gender, age group, or profession. Understanding these connections allows law enforcement to narrow their focus and anticipate the killer's next potential target. Victimology also helps investigators understand the killer's motives and psychological profile, further aiding in linking crimes.

Geographic profiling is another powerful tool in tracking patterns. This method analyzes the locations of murders to identify spatial patterns that reveal the killer's hunting grounds and potential base of operations. Serial killers often operate within a comfort zone, committing crimes in areas they know well. By mapping crime scenes and examining the distances between them, investigators can predict where the killer might live or work. Geographic profiling also helps identify clusters of activity, allowing law enforcement to concentrate resources in areas where the killer is most likely to strike again.

Data-sharing systems and databases have transformed how police link murders across jurisdictions. Tools like the FBI's Violent Criminal Apprehension Program (ViCAP) allow law enforcement agencies to input details about crimes, including MOs, victim characteristics, and forensic evidence, into a centralized database. These systems analyze the data to identify similarities between cases, connecting crimes that might otherwise remain isolated due to jurisdictional boundaries. This level of collaboration is particularly important for catching killers who operate across state or national lines, exploiting gaps in communication between local agencies.

Technological advancements have further enhanced the ability to track patterns and link murders. Facial recognition software, license plate readers, and cellphone tracking are used to identify suspects and place them near crime scenes. Digital footprints, such as internet search histories, social media activity, or GPS data, can reveal connections between suspects and victims or indicate premeditation. Advances in machine learning and artificial intelligence also play a growing role, with algorithms analyzing large datasets to detect patterns and correlations that might elude human investigators.

Public involvement and media play an important role in tracking patterns as well. Tip lines, public appeals, and media coverage can generate leads, identify additional victims, or bring forward witnesses who were unaware of the significance of their information. Killers who seek notoriety, like the Zodiac Killer or Dennis Rader (BTK), often leave clues or communicate with law enforcement, unintentionally providing critical information that helps link their crimes.

Ultimately, tracking patterns and linking murders requires a multidisciplinary approach, combining science, psychology, and technology with traditional investigative methods. It involves piecing together small details—consistent injuries, geographic overlaps, victim similarities, and ritualistic behaviors—into a larger picture that reveals the identity and methods of the killer. The process not only helps solve individual cases but also creates a deeper understanding of serial crime, allowing law enforcement to predict and prevent future murders. By recognizing and analyzing these patterns, police can turn fragmented evidence into a coherent narrative that leads to the apprehension of some of the most elusive criminals.

# Chapter 11: Inside the Interview Room

## What Serial Killers Reveal

Interrogating serial killers is one of the most complex and psychologically demanding tasks for investigators. Serial killers are often manipulative, calculating, and highly resistant to revealing the truth. To counter this, law enforcement employs carefully crafted psychological strategies designed to break down their defenses, build rapport, and elicit confessions or critical details about their crimes. The interrogation of a serial killer is as much about understanding their mindset as it is about uncovering the facts, and the process often reveals chilling insights into their behavior and motivations.

One of the key strategies used in these interviews is the establishment of rapport. Despite the heinous nature of their crimes, serial killers often crave recognition and validation. Interrogators leverage this by creating an atmosphere of understanding, allowing the killer to feel that their actions and intelligence are being acknowledged. This approach minimizes hostility and encourages the killer to open up. For example, an investigator might express curiosity about the killer's methods or motivations, subtly appealing to their ego and need for attention. Building rapport requires patience and psychological acumen, as it often takes time for a killer to trust the interrogator enough to share details of their crimes.

Another common strategy is mirroring the killer's behavior. Serial killers are adept at reading people and often test the boundaries of their interrogators. To counter this, investigators may adopt a calm, nonjudgmental demeanor that mirrors the killer's emotional state. This approach prevents the killer from feeling threatened or judged, making them more likely to engage in conversation. For instance, if a killer presents themselves as unemotional or detached, the interrogator might respond in kind, creating a neutral environment that encourages dialogue. This tactic can be particularly effective with psychopathic offenders, who are more likely to respond to logic and curiosity than to displays of emotion.

Exploiting narcissism is another critical tactic in interrogations. Many serial killers, such as Ted Bundy and Dennis Rader, possess inflated egos and a belief in their own superiority. Investigators often appeal to this sense of self-importance by framing questions in a way that highlights the killer's intelligence or uniqueness. For example, an interrogator might ask, "How did you manage to avoid capture for so long?" or "What makes you different from others who have committed similar crimes?" These questions feed the killer's ego and encourage them to boast about their actions, inadvertently providing valuable information about their methods and motives.

Gradual confrontation is used to challenge inconsistencies in the killer's narrative without triggering defensiveness. Serial killers are often skilled liars, capable of constructing elaborate stories to deflect suspicion. Instead of directly accusing the killer of lying, interrogators introduce evidence incrementally, guiding the conversation toward contradictions in their statements. This method allows the killer to feel as though they are revealing information on their own terms, making them less likely to shut down or become combative. For example, if a killer denies being at a crime scene, an investigator might first present circumstantial evidence, such as witness sightings, before introducing more definitive proof like DNA or video footage.

Understanding and leveraging psychological vulnerabilities is another powerful tool in the interrogation room. Serial killers are not immune to fear, guilt, or emotional triggers, even if they appear detached or remorseless. Investigators often identify and exploit these vulnerabilities to create pressure. For example, a killer who shows signs of regret or mentions their family might be reminded of how their actions have impacted loved ones. Similarly, religious killers might be confronted with moral or spiritual consequences, appealing to their belief systems. These techniques are carefully tailored to the individual, based on the psychological profile developed during the investigation.

Interrogators also use silence and nonverbal cues to their advantage. Many serial killers, especially those who crave control, are uncomfortable with silence and will attempt to fill the void by speaking. This tactic, known as the "silent treatment," can prompt killers to reveal information they had not intended to share. Additionally, nonverbal cues such as sustained eye contact, a relaxed posture, or subtle nods are used to convey authority and attentiveness, encouraging the killer to continue talking. These small but deliberate actions create an environment where the killer feels both observed and compelled to respond.

Strategic storytelling is another effective technique. By recounting scenarios similar to the killer's crimes, investigators can elicit reactions that reveal guilt or knowledge. For example, an interrogator might describe a hypothetical murder and ask the killer how they think the perpetrator might have felt or acted. This approach allows the killer to project their own experiences without directly incriminating themselves, providing valuable insights into their thought processes. Over time, these projections can evolve into confessions as the killer becomes more comfortable discussing their crimes.

Finally, investigators often employ psychological profiling to anticipate the killer's responses. Before the interrogation, profilers analyze the killer's personality, background, and motivations to predict their behavior in the interview room. This preparation allows interrogators to tailor their approach, choosing strategies that are most likely to resonate with the individual. For example, a killer who thrives on control may be given the illusion of power in the conversation, while a remorseful killer might be approached with empathy to encourage confession. Profiling ensures that each interrogation is as effective as possible, maximizing the chances of uncovering critical information.

The insights gained during these interrogations often reveal not only the mechanics of the crimes but also the psychological depths of the killer's mind. Serial killers may describe their motivations, fantasies, and emotions in unsettling detail, shedding light on the complex interplay of factors that drove their actions. While the interrogation process is fraught with challenges, it remains one of the most effective ways to uncover the truth and provide closure for victims' families. These interviews are more than just a means of solving cases—they are a window into the darkest corners of human behavior, offering valuable lessons for both investigators and society at large.

### Confessions, manipulations, and the lies they tell

Serial killers are often master manipulators, and their confessions, lies, and manipulative tactics serve as tools to control the narrative and protect their sense of power. In the interrogation room, what they reveal—or withhold—provides insight into their psychology while posing significant challenges for investigators. Their confessions can be calculated, their lies elaborate, and their manipulations designed to maintain dominance, even when caught.

Confessions from serial killers are rarely straightforward admissions of guilt. Many killers only confess to crimes when they believe it serves their interests, whether to gain notoriety, manipulate law enforcement, or avoid harsher punishment. Some, like Ted Bundy, offered confessions strategically, using them as bargaining chips to delay execution or to gain attention. These confessions often include selective truths, as killers reveal just enough to seem cooperative while withholding key details to retain control. For example, they may admit to certain murders but omit others, forcing investigators to continue pursuing answers on the killer's terms.

Even when serial killers confess, their admissions are often steeped in self-serving narratives. They may downplay their crimes, blame external factors, or present themselves as victims of circumstance. Killers like Aileen Wuornos framed their actions as acts of self-defense, casting themselves as protectors rather than predators. Others may confess in a way that glorifies their intelligence or cunning, relishing the opportunity to recount their crimes as stories of superiority. This allows them to preserve their ego while providing investigators with selective information that aligns with their preferred image.

Manipulation is a hallmark of serial killers, and their interactions with law enforcement are no exception. In interviews, they often attempt to control the pace and direction of the conversation, using charm, deflection, or intimidation. Killers like John Wayne Gacy, for instance, maintained an outwardly cooperative demeanor, offering plausible explanations for evidence while steering investigators away from his crimes. This manipulation extends to how they present themselves, with many killers adopting personas that mask their true nature. They may appear calm, articulate, or even remorseful to disarm investigators, creating a false sense of trust.

Serial killers are also adept at crafting lies that serve their psychological needs or protect their interests. Their lies often reflect their intelligence and ability to manipulate facts, weaving elaborate stories to mislead investigators. For example, they might fabricate alibis, shift blame onto others, or invent justifications for their actions. These lies are not merely attempts to avoid detection; they are also a means of asserting control over the situation. By deceiving law enforcement, killers reinforce their belief in their own superiority, even in the face of overwhelming evidence.

The lies told by serial killers often extend to their motives, as they seek to obscure the true nature of their crimes. Some may claim altruistic intentions, presenting their actions as necessary or justified. Others fabricate motivations that align with societal fears or myths, such as claiming to act under the influence of a cult or supernatural forces. These false narratives not only deflect attention from their actual motives but also serve to create intrigue and confusion, ensuring their crimes remain the subject of public fascination.

In some cases, serial killers use confessions and lies as a means of maintaining relevance and control after their capture. Killers like Israel Keyes withheld details about their crimes, doling out information slowly to prolong their interactions with law enforcement. This drip-feeding of confessions keeps investigators engaged and reinforces the killer's sense of power, as they remain the sole source of information about their actions. This tactic can also be used to manipulate outcomes, such as negotiating for privileges or avoiding certain punishments.

Serial killers' lies are often layered with elements of truth, making them particularly challenging to unravel. Investigators must sift through their statements carefully, separating fact from fiction to piece together an accurate account of events. Behavioral analysis plays a crucial role in this process, as law enforcement examines the killer's body language, tone, and emotional responses to identify inconsistencies or signs of deception. This meticulous work is essential, as the lies of serial killers can obscure vital details about their crimes or even lead to the wrongful implication of others.

Confessions, manipulations, and lies are not just tactics for serial killers; they are extensions of their need for control and dominance. Even when faced with overwhelming evidence, they rarely relinquish their power willingly, instead using every interaction as an opportunity to assert their superiority. Understanding these behaviors is critical for investigators, as it provides insight into the psychological drivers behind the crimes while equipping law enforcement with strategies to counter their manipulative tactics. Ultimately, the stories serial killers tell—whether truthful or fabricated—offer a window into their minds, revealing the complexities and contradictions of their twisted realities.

# Insights from interviews with convicted serial killers

Interviews with convicted serial killers provide a rare and unsettling glimpse into the minds of some of the world's most dangerous individuals. These conversations, conducted by law enforcement, psychologists, and researchers, often reveal key insights into their motivations, psychological processes, and the factors that shaped their violent behavior. While each killer is unique, patterns and commonalities often emerge, offering valuable lessons for criminal investigations, psychological profiling, and understanding the darker aspects of human behavior.

One of the most striking insights gained from these interviews is the role of fantasy in driving serial killers' actions. Many convicted killers describe how their violent impulses began as vivid, recurring fantasies that grew more elaborate over time. These mental scenarios often involved themes of power, control, and domination, with the eventual act of killing serving as an attempt to bring these fantasies to life. For example, killers like Dennis Rader (BTK) and Jeffrey Dahmer openly discussed how their fantasies fueled their crimes, detailing the gratification they sought by turning imagined scenarios into reality. These confessions highlight the connection between unchecked fantasies and the escalation to violence.

Another common theme revealed in interviews is the killers' lack of empathy and emotional detachment from their victims. Many serial killers view their victims not as people but as objects or symbols, reducing them to tools for fulfilling their own needs. Ted Bundy, for instance, described how he compartmentalized his crimes, rationalizing his actions and avoiding emotional connection to his victims. This detachment allows killers to commit horrific acts without guilt, and their interviews often reveal chilling indifference when recounting their crimes. Understanding this emotional void has been crucial for profiling, as it highlights the absence of typical moral constraints in serial offenders.

Interviews also frequently uncover a deep-seated need for power and control. Serial killers often describe how their crimes gave them a sense of dominance over their victims, allowing them to assert authority and compensate for feelings of inadequacy in their own lives. John Wayne Gacy spoke about how his murders allowed him to maintain control in ways he couldn't in other aspects of his life. This need for power is not limited to the act of killing; many killers derive satisfaction from the planning and manipulation involved in luring their victims, reflecting their desire to dominate every stage of the crime.

Trauma and early life experiences are another recurring topic in interviews with serial killers. Many have detailed histories of abuse, neglect, or rejection, which they cite as pivotal moments in shaping their worldview and violent tendencies. Aileen Wuornos, for example, spoke extensively about her abusive upbringing and how it influenced her rage and distrust of others, particularly men. These interviews highlight how early experiences of victimization can distort a person's emotional development, leading to cycles of violence and revenge. However, it's important to note that while trauma may play a role, it does not fully explain why some individuals become serial killers while others with similar experiences do not.

Interviews with serial killers also provide insights into their manipulative tendencies. Many killers describe how they used charm, deceit, or intimidation to gain the trust of their victims or evade capture. Ted Bundy famously used his charisma and feigned vulnerability—such as pretending to have a broken arm—to lure victims into his control. This ability to manipulate others extends to their interactions with law enforcement and interviewers, as they often seek to control the narrative or present themselves in a way that aligns with their desired image. These behaviors underscore their skill at deception and their need to maintain a sense of superiority, even after their crimes are exposed.

One particularly valuable aspect of these interviews is the opportunity to understand how serial killers view themselves. Many display a distorted sense of reality, rationalizing their actions or framing themselves as victims of circumstance. Some, like Richard Ramirez (the Night Stalker), embraced their notoriety, reveling in the fear and infamy they created. Others, such as Edmund Kemper, offered self-reflective insights into their own pathology, acknowledging their violent tendencies and the psychological factors that drove them. These self-perceptions provide critical data for understanding the mindset of serial offenders and the narratives they construct to justify their actions.

Interviews often reveal the role of escalation in their behavior. Many killers describe how their first crime was a pivotal moment that failed to satisfy their fantasies fully, leading to a compulsion to kill again in search of the "perfect" experience. This escalation is marked by increasing violence, frequency, or ritualistic elements, as killers refine their methods and attempt to fulfill their psychological needs. Jeffrey Dahmer, for instance, spoke about how his crimes became increasingly elaborate as he sought to create compliant victims who would never leave him, reflecting his deep-seated fears of abandonment and loneliness.

These conversations also highlight the importance of forensic psychology and behavioral analysis in criminal investigations. By studying the accounts of convicted serial killers, investigators and psychologists have developed more accurate profiles of offenders, identifying patterns in behavior, victim selection, and crime scene evidence. This knowledge has been instrumental in solving cases and preventing future crimes, as it provides law enforcement with a deeper understanding of how serial killers think and operate.

Despite their value, interviews with serial killers are fraught with challenges. Many offenders are skilled liars who use these opportunities to manipulate or mislead, making it essential for interviewers to approach with skepticism and psychological expertise. However, when conducted effectively, these interviews provide unparalleled insights into the minds of serial killers, shedding light on their motivations, methods, and psychological makeup. By studying these accounts, society can better understand and address the conditions that allow such individuals to emerge, ultimately working to prevent future tragedies.

# Chapter 12: The Aftermath

## Effects on Victims, Families, and Communities

The aftermath of serial killings leaves an indelible mark on survivors, victims' families, and entire communities. The trauma endured by those affected is profound, multifaceted, and often long-lasting, reshaping lives in ways that extend far beyond the immediate aftermath of the crimes. This trauma manifests in emotional, psychological, and even physical ways, as those left behind struggle to make sense of the violence and reclaim a sense of safety and stability.

For survivors of serial killers—those who manage to escape or survive an attack—the experience is often life-altering. Many grapple with post-traumatic stress disorder (PTSD), characterized by flashbacks, nightmares, and a heightened sense of fear and vigilance. Survivors may feel intense guilt for having survived when others did not, a phenomenon known as survivor's guilt. This emotional burden can lead to feelings of isolation, as they struggle to communicate their experience to others who may not fully understand the depth of their pain. Additionally, survivors often face physical injuries or disfigurement that serve as constant reminders of their trauma, further complicating their recovery.

For the families of victims, the loss is compounded by the violent nature of the crime and the public attention it often receives. Unlike natural deaths, murders committed by serial killers are frequently sensationalized by the media, forcing families to relive their pain as their loved one's name and story are repeatedly discussed. This intrusion into their grief can delay the healing process, as families are unable to mourn privately. Many families also experience a sense of helplessness and anger, particularly if the killer evades capture for an extended period. The uncertainty and lack of closure can lead to long-term emotional distress, with families living in a state of unresolved grief.

Even when a killer is caught, the legal process can prolong the trauma for victims' families. Trials often require families to hear graphic details about their loved one's death, sometimes directly from the killer. While justice may bring a sense of resolution, it rarely alleviates the pain of loss. Some families channel their grief into advocacy, working to support other victims or push for legal reforms, but this path is not without its emotional toll. For many, the trauma becomes a defining aspect of their lives, altering relationships, careers, and mental health.

The impact of serial killings extends beyond individuals to entire communities, especially when the crimes remain unsolved for a significant period. Fear and paranoia often grip affected areas, with residents feeling unsafe in their own neighborhoods. Community members may alter their routines, avoid certain areas, or live in constant vigilance, unsure of who might be the next target. This pervasive fear can strain community cohesion, as suspicion grows and trust erodes among neighbors. In extreme cases, the stigma associated with serial killings can tarnish a community's reputation, impacting local businesses, tourism, and property values.

Communities also experience secondary trauma as they process the violence and grapple with their inability to prevent it. This is particularly true in cases where systemic failures, such as poor policing or societal neglect of vulnerable populations, contributed to the killer's ability to operate undetected. For example, communities where serial killers targeted marginalized groups, such as sex workers or racial minorities, may confront difficult questions about societal biases and the lack of resources devoted to protecting those groups. These broader issues add another layer of complexity to the collective trauma experienced by the community.

The media's role in amplifying the aftermath cannot be understated. While coverage can help raise awareness and pressure law enforcement to act, it often sensationalizes the killer rather than focusing on the victims and their families. This narrative shift can leave survivors and families feeling sidelined, as the focus moves away from their grief to the killer's psychology or notoriety. Efforts to humanize victims and prioritize their stories are essential to counteract this imbalance and ensure that their lives, rather than their deaths, remain the central narrative.

Support systems play a crucial role in helping survivors, families, and communities recover. Counseling and therapy are essential for addressing the deep psychological wounds caused by the trauma, providing a safe space to process emotions and rebuild a sense of normalcy. Support groups for families of murder victims can also offer solace, as shared experiences create a sense of understanding and solidarity. For communities, collective healing efforts, such as vigils, memorials, and public discussions, can foster a sense of resilience and unity, reminding residents that they are not defined by the violence but by their ability to come together in its aftermath.

Ultimately, the trauma caused by serial killings is a ripple effect that touches everyone connected to the crimes, from direct survivors to distant community members. The scars it leaves are deep, but with the right resources, understanding, and support, healing is possible. By acknowledging the long-term impact on victims, families, and communities, society can work to provide the care and compassion needed to rebuild lives while striving to prevent such tragedies from occurring in the future.

**How communities respond and rebuild after serial killings**

Communities respond and rebuild after serial killings through a combination of mourning, resilience, and collective action aimed at restoring safety, trust, and a sense of normalcy. Serial killings leave deep psychological and emotional scars on affected communities, disrupting the daily lives of residents and eroding their sense of security. The process of rebuilding is complex and multifaceted, requiring time, resources, and a unified effort to overcome the fear and trauma left in the wake of such crimes.

One of the immediate ways communities respond is through collective mourning. Vigils, memorials, and public gatherings are often organized to honor the victims and provide a space for shared grief. These events allow residents to come together in solidarity, offering support to one another and to the victims' families. The act of collectively acknowledging the tragedy fosters a sense of unity and helps to counter the isolation and fear that often follow serial killings. These moments of remembrance also serve as an important first step in the healing process, reminding community members of their shared humanity and resilience.

Strengthening community bonds is another critical aspect of rebuilding. Serial killings often create an atmosphere of suspicion, where residents may become wary of neighbors or avoid public spaces. To counter this, many communities prioritize rebuilding trust through open communication and collaboration. Neighborhood watch programs, town hall meetings, and community outreach initiatives are frequently implemented to encourage residents to reconnect and work together to ensure safety. These efforts not only help restore a sense of security but also empower individuals to take an active role in protecting their community.

Improving local law enforcement practices is a key focus in the aftermath of serial killings. When a killer operates undetected for an extended period, it often exposes gaps in police resources, communication, or investigative methods. Communities may demand reforms, such as better funding for law enforcement, improved inter-agency coordination, or the establishment of specialized investigative units. The implementation of these changes helps restore public confidence in law enforcement while addressing systemic vulnerabilities that may have allowed the crimes to continue unchecked.

Public education and awareness campaigns also play a vital role in the rebuilding process. These initiatives aim to inform residents about personal safety, crime prevention, and how to recognize warning signs of predatory behavior. Schools, workplaces, and community organizations often participate in these campaigns, equipping individuals with the knowledge and tools needed to protect themselves and others. By empowering residents with information, these efforts foster a sense of control and resilience, countering the fear and helplessness that serial killings often instill.

Mental health support is another essential component of community recovery. The trauma of serial killings can have far-reaching psychological effects, not only on the victims' families but also on residents who may feel unsafe or emotionally impacted by the crimes. Counseling services, support groups, and crisis hotlines are often established to address these needs, providing individuals with a safe space to process their emotions and begin healing. Mental health professionals also play a crucial role in helping communities understand the broader impact of trauma and develop strategies for resilience.

Media coverage can both help and hinder community recovery. While responsible reporting can raise awareness and provide important updates on the investigation, sensationalized or fear-driven narratives can prolong anxiety and stigmatize the affected area. Communities often respond by reclaiming their narrative, focusing on stories of resilience, remembrance, and progress rather than the notoriety of the killer. Efforts to highlight the lives of the victims, celebrate acts of kindness, and emphasize the community's strength in the face of tragedy help to shift the focus from fear to hope.

The rebuilding process also involves creating lasting legacies that honor the victims and promote positive change. Communities may establish scholarships, foundations, or charitable initiatives in the names of the victims, turning their memory into a force for good. These efforts not only preserve the victims' legacies but also provide a sense of purpose and direction for the community, demonstrating that even in the face of tragedy, positive outcomes can emerge.

Ultimately, how a community responds and rebuilds after serial killings reflects its resilience and determination to heal. While the scars of such events may never fully fade, the collective efforts of residents, law enforcement, and support networks ensure that the community can move forward stronger and more united. Through mourning, reform, education, and empowerment, communities prove that even in the wake of the darkest events, hope and recovery are possible.

**The broader societal implications of serial crimes**
The broader societal implications of serial crimes extend far beyond the immediate victims and their families, influencing cultural norms, public policy, law enforcement practices, and the collective psyche. Serial killings are not only horrific acts of violence but also societal events that challenge perceptions of safety, expose systemic vulnerabilities, and ignite debates about human behavior, justice, and morality. These crimes reveal deep-seated issues within communities and institutions, prompting widespread reflection and often leading to long-term changes in how society addresses violence and security.

One of the most immediate societal implications of serial crimes is the heightened sense of fear and vulnerability they create. Serial killings disrupt the perception of safety within communities, replacing a sense of security with uncertainty and mistrust. This fear can spread rapidly through media coverage, affecting not just those in the immediate vicinity of the crimes but also people far removed from the events. Serial crimes tap into primal fears of being targeted by an unseen predator, and this psychological impact often persists long after the killer is caught. The widespread anxiety generated by such crimes can influence behavior, leading individuals to alter routines, avoid public spaces, or take additional security measures.

Serial crimes also expose societal inequalities and vulnerabilities, particularly in how certain groups are targeted and how their victimization is addressed. Many serial killers prey on marginalized individuals, such as sex workers, homeless people, or racial minorities, whose disappearances may not receive the same level of attention or urgency from law enforcement. This disparity highlights systemic biases and gaps in the protection of vulnerable populations, sparking discussions about the need for equitable justice and societal reforms. Cases like those of the Green River Killer, who primarily targeted sex workers, have drawn attention to how societal stigmas can delay investigations and allow killers to operate unchecked.

The cultural fascination with serial killers also has significant implications for how society processes and understands these crimes. True crime media, including books, documentaries, and podcasts, often sensationalizes serial killers, sometimes elevating them to near-mythical status. While these portrayals can provide valuable insights into criminal psychology and law enforcement, they also risk glorifying the killers, overshadowing the victims, and perpetuating harmful stereotypes. This fascination reflects a broader societal struggle to reconcile the allure of the macabre with the need to honor and humanize those who suffered.

On a policy level, serial crimes frequently lead to reforms in law enforcement and criminal justice practices. High-profile cases have spurred the creation of centralized databases, such as the FBI's ViCAP system, to track and connect violent crimes across jurisdictions. These tools have revolutionized how law enforcement identifies and apprehends serial offenders, highlighting the importance of collaboration and data sharing.

Serial crimes have also prompted advancements in forensic technology, including DNA analysis and geographic profiling, which have become essential in solving not only active cases but also decades-old cold cases. The societal demand for justice and accountability in the wake of serial crimes has driven these innovations, reshaping investigative practices on a global scale.

The psychological and sociological study of serial killers has further influenced societal understanding of human behavior and mental health. These crimes have fueled research into the causes of violent behavior, exploring the interplay of genetics, environment, and trauma. This has led to greater awareness of early warning signs, such as the "Macdonald Triad" (animal cruelty, fire-setting, and bed-wetting), as well as the impact of childhood abuse and neglect. While not all individuals with these traits become violent, the study of serial killers has underscored the importance of addressing mental health issues and providing intervention before they escalate into dangerous behavior.

Serial crimes also challenge societal perceptions of morality, justice, and punishment. Public reactions to these crimes often vary, with some advocating for harsher penalties and others focusing on rehabilitation or understanding the root causes of violence. The debates surrounding the death penalty, for example, are frequently reignited by cases involving serial killers, as society grapples with the ethical and practical implications of capital punishment. These discussions force society to confront difficult questions about retribution, forgiveness, and the nature of evil.

Another societal implication of serial crimes is their impact on trust in institutions. When serial killers evade capture for extended periods, it often exposes weaknesses in law enforcement, government oversight, or social services. High-profile cases can lead to public scrutiny of these institutions, resulting in demands for accountability and reform. For instance, the failure to apprehend killers like Jack the Ripper or the Zodiac Killer for decades has highlighted the challenges of investigative work, while also fostering skepticism about institutional competence. This erosion of trust can have far-reaching effects, influencing how communities view authority and engage with public systems.

Despite the fear and disruption caused by serial crimes, they also have the potential to unite society in collective action. Communities affected by these crimes often rally together, creating support networks, advocating for victims, and pushing for systemic change. The legacy of serial crimes, while rooted in tragedy, can inspire progress and resilience, as society learns from its failures and works to prevent similar events in the future. These efforts reflect the broader human capacity to find meaning and strength in the face of adversity, transforming even the darkest chapters of history into opportunities for growth and improvement.

Ultimately, the societal implications of serial crimes are profound and multifaceted, touching every aspect of culture, policy, and public consciousness. These events force society to confront its vulnerabilities, question its values, and adapt its systems to better protect its members. While the impact of serial crimes is deeply painful, the lessons they impart serve as a catalyst for change, ensuring that the victims and their stories leave a lasting mark on the world.

# Chapter 13: Can Monsters Be Made?

## Examining the Rehabilitation Debate

The question of whether serial killers can be rehabilitated is one of the most polarizing and complex issues in criminal justice and psychology. Serial killers are often perceived as "monsters," individuals whose violent actions and lack of empathy seem beyond the reach of change or redemption. Their crimes evoke intense public outrage and a demand for justice, leaving little room for discussions about rehabilitation. However, as researchers delve deeper into the psychological and environmental factors that contribute to serial killings, the debate over whether these individuals are born or shaped—and whether they can be reformed—becomes increasingly nuanced.

Those who argue against the possibility of rehabilitation often point to the psychological profiles of serial killers. Many exhibit traits associated with psychopathy, such as a lack of empathy, an inability to feel remorse, and a manipulative nature. These traits, particularly when coupled with deeply ingrained patterns of violent behavior, make the prospect of rehabilitation seem unlikely. Critics argue that the compulsive nature of serial killers' actions, driven by fantasies or an insatiable need for control, makes them resistant to traditional therapeutic approaches. They contend that efforts to rehabilitate such individuals risk endangering society, as any failure in treatment could lead to further violence.

The biological and neurological factors associated with serial killers also fuel skepticism about rehabilitation. Research has shown that some serial killers display abnormalities in brain structures associated with impulse control, emotional regulation, and moral reasoning, such as the prefrontal cortex and amygdala. These findings suggest that certain aspects of their behavior may be hardwired, raising questions about whether therapy or other interventions can truly alter their capacity for violence. For many, these biological predispositions reinforce the belief that serial killers cannot be rehabilitated and should instead be permanently removed from society through incarceration or capital punishment.

On the other hand, proponents of rehabilitation argue that serial killers, like all individuals, are products of their environment and experiences. Many serial killers have histories of severe trauma, abuse, or neglect, which shaped their worldview and contributed to their violent behavior. Advocates for rehabilitation emphasize that understanding and addressing these root causes can pave the way for therapeutic interventions. They point to cases where violent offenders—though not necessarily serial killers—have shown progress through intensive therapy, suggesting that change is possible with the right approach.

Cognitive-behavioral therapy (CBT) and other evidence-based treatments have been used successfully with certain types of offenders, focusing on changing thought patterns and behaviors. While the application of these methods to serial killers is limited, some psychologists believe that structured, long-term therapy could help reduce violent tendencies or at least manage the impulses that drive their behavior. The idea is not necessarily to reform serial killers into fully functioning members of society but to mitigate the risk of future harm by addressing the underlying psychological issues.

The ethical dimension of the rehabilitation debate is equally complex. Critics often question whether serial killers deserve the resources and effort required for rehabilitation, given the enormity of their crimes. They argue that these individuals have forfeited their right to second chances by committing acts of unimaginable cruelty. Supporters of rehabilitation, however, contend that the goal of the justice system should be more than punishment. They argue that if there is even a small chance of reforming a serial killer and preventing future violence, society has a moral obligation to explore that possibility.

The potential for rehabilitation also raises practical concerns about public safety. Even if a serial killer were to show progress in therapy, the risk of reoffending would remain a significant concern. The nature of their crimes and the difficulty in fully assessing their psychological state make it nearly impossible to guarantee that they would not revert to violent behavior. This uncertainty makes the prospect of releasing a rehabilitated serial killer into society an unacceptable risk for many.

Despite the contentious nature of the debate, examining the possibility of rehabilitation for serial killers provides valuable insights into the broader question of how society understands and responds to violence. It challenges us to consider the balance between punishment and compassion, the role of science in addressing human behavior, and the limits of what can be achieved through intervention. Whether or not serial killers can truly be rehabilitated, the debate underscores the importance of prevention, early intervention, and addressing the systemic issues that contribute to the creation of violent offenders.

Ultimately, the question of whether monsters can be made or unmade remains unresolved. Serial killers occupy a unique and deeply troubling space in the human psyche, their actions defying easy explanation or solutions. While the debate over rehabilitation may never yield a definitive answer, it continues to push the boundaries of our understanding of criminal behavior, the nature of evil, and the potential for change. In exploring these questions, society gains not only a deeper understanding of serial killers but also a greater awareness of its own capacity for justice, mercy, and accountability.

## Can therapy or medication alter the behavior of violent offenders?

The question of whether therapy or medication can alter the behavior of violent offenders is a deeply debated issue, intersecting psychology, neuroscience, and criminal justice. While some violent offenders respond positively to treatment, the effectiveness of these interventions depends on various factors, including the individual's psychological profile, the root causes of their violent behavior, and the type of therapy or medication used. For certain offenders, therapy and medication have proven to be valuable tools in reducing aggression and managing impulses, but their application and success are far from universal.

Therapy is one of the most commonly used approaches for addressing violent behavior, with cognitive-behavioral therapy (CBT) being particularly prominent. CBT focuses on identifying and altering thought patterns and behaviors that contribute to aggression. For example, it helps offenders recognize triggers for their violence, develop coping mechanisms, and replace destructive responses with healthier ones. CBT has shown success in reducing recidivism rates among some offenders, particularly those whose violence stems from learned behaviors or poor impulse control. Programs like anger management or conflict resolution, often rooted in CBT principles, are designed to help individuals process emotions constructively and mitigate violent tendencies.

Another therapeutic approach is trauma-focused therapy, which addresses the role of past experiences in shaping violent behavior. Many violent offenders have histories of abuse, neglect, or other forms of trauma that contribute to their actions. Therapies like eye movement desensitization and reprocessing (EMDR) or prolonged exposure therapy aim to help individuals process and heal from these traumatic experiences. By addressing the root causes of their behavior, trauma-focused therapy can reduce the emotional and psychological drivers of violence, though its effectiveness varies widely based on the individual's willingness to engage in the process.

Medication also plays a role in altering the behavior of violent offenders, particularly when their actions are linked to underlying mental health disorders or neurological conditions. For instance, antipsychotic medications are often used to manage violent behavior in individuals with schizophrenia or other psychotic disorders, where aggression may stem from delusions or paranoia. Similarly, mood stabilizers like lithium or anticonvulsants are prescribed to individuals with bipolar disorder or other conditions involving mood dysregulation, helping to reduce impulsivity and aggression.

Selective serotonin reuptake inhibitors (SSRIs), commonly used to treat depression and anxiety, have also been shown to reduce aggression in some cases. By regulating serotonin levels in the brain, these medications can improve emotional regulation and decrease violent outbursts. However, the effectiveness of medication varies significantly between individuals, and the wrong prescription or dosage can exacerbate problems rather than alleviate them. Medication alone is rarely a complete solution; it is most effective when combined with therapy and other interventions.

Despite the potential benefits, the limitations of therapy and medication in altering violent behavior must be acknowledged. For individuals with deeply ingrained patterns of violence, such as serial killers or psychopathic offenders, traditional therapeutic approaches may be ineffective. Psychopaths, for example, often exhibit traits like a lack of empathy, remorse, or emotional depth, which can make them resistant to therapy. In some cases, therapy may even enable them to become more manipulative by teaching them how to better mimic socially acceptable behavior without addressing their underlying tendencies.

Compliance is another significant challenge, particularly with medication. Many offenders struggle with maintaining consistent use of prescribed medications, whether due to side effects, distrust of the system, or a lack of access to resources. Without consistent adherence, the benefits of medication are diminished, and the risk of violent behavior returning increases. Furthermore, therapy requires a willingness to engage and change, which some violent offenders lack. For individuals who are unwilling or unable to reflect on their behavior, therapy may provide little benefit.

The effectiveness of these interventions also depends on the context in which they are delivered. Incarceration environments, for instance, often lack the resources or trained professionals needed to provide effective therapeutic programs.

Overcrowding, limited funding, and punitive attitudes toward rehabilitation can undermine the success of treatment efforts. Conversely, offenders who receive therapy and medication in structured, supportive environments are more likely to experience positive outcomes.

Ultimately, while therapy and medication can alter the behavior of some violent offenders, they are not universally effective and must be tailored to the individual. Success depends on addressing the root causes of violence, the offender's willingness to participate, and the availability of appropriate resources. A combination of therapeutic and pharmacological interventions, supported by long-term monitoring and societal reintegration programs, offers the best chance of reducing violent tendencies. However, for certain individuals—particularly those with severe psychopathy or entrenched patterns of violence—the potential for meaningful behavioral change remains limited. This underscores the need for continued research, innovation, and a nuanced approach to addressing violent behavior in society.

### The role of mental institutions versus the penal system

The role of mental institutions versus the penal system in addressing criminal behavior has long been a topic of debate, as these two systems serve distinct yet overlapping purposes. Mental institutions focus on treatment and rehabilitation for individuals with psychological disorders, while the penal system emphasizes punishment, deterrence, and public safety. Determining which system is more appropriate for violent offenders, particularly those with mental health issues, requires a nuanced understanding of the interplay between mental illness and criminal behavior.

Mental institutions are designed to address the root causes of behavior through therapeutic interventions, medication, and structured care. They prioritize treatment over punishment, operating under the belief that addressing underlying psychological issues can reduce the risk of reoffending. For individuals whose crimes are driven by severe mental illness—such as schizophrenia, bipolar disorder, or psychosis—mental institutions provide an environment tailored to their needs. Patients in these settings receive comprehensive evaluations, individualized treatment plans, and access to psychiatric care, which are often unavailable in the penal system. The goal is to stabilize their mental health, manage symptoms, and, where possible, reintegrate them into society.

In contrast, the penal system prioritizes accountability and public safety. Prisons are structured to remove offenders from society, often without addressing the underlying factors that contributed to their crimes. While many correctional facilities offer mental health services, these resources are often limited, underfunded, or inadequate for addressing complex psychological issues. This lack of comprehensive care means that offenders with untreated mental health conditions may experience worsening symptoms while incarcerated, potentially leading to further behavioral problems or violent outbursts. The punitive nature of the penal system often exacerbates the struggles of individuals with mental illness, as the environment can be isolating, stressful, and even retraumatizing.

One of the key distinctions between mental institutions and the penal system is their approach to rehabilitation. Mental institutions operate with the goal of recovery and reintegration, providing patients with tools to manage their conditions and reduce the likelihood of future violence. This includes therapy, education, and life skills training, all aimed at improving the individual's ability to function in society. In contrast, the penal system often emphasizes punishment over rehabilitation, with limited opportunities for offenders to address the factors that led to their crimes. This punitive approach can perpetuate cycles of reoffending, as individuals leave prison without the support or skills needed to avoid criminal behavior.

For individuals who commit crimes due to mental illness, placement in a mental institution rather than a prison can significantly impact their outcomes. Studies have shown that offenders with severe mental health conditions who receive appropriate treatment are less likely to reoffend than those who are incarcerated without access to care. Mental institutions also provide a more humane alternative to incarceration, recognizing that mental illness is often a driving factor behind criminal behavior. However, public perception and policy often lean toward punishment, particularly for violent crimes, which can limit the availability of mental health-based alternatives.

Despite their distinct roles, mental institutions and the penal system are not mutually exclusive. In some cases, a hybrid approach is necessary, such as forensic psychiatric facilities that bridge the gap between treatment and security. These institutions are designed for individuals deemed mentally unfit for traditional incarceration but who pose a significant risk to public safety. Forensic facilities provide intensive psychiatric care in a secure environment, ensuring that both the individual's needs and societal concerns are addressed. This model offers a potential solution for balancing the goals of rehabilitation and accountability.

The debate over the appropriate use of mental institutions versus the penal system also raises broader questions about how society views mental illness and criminal responsibility. Critics of the penal system argue that it often criminalizes mental illness, as individuals with untreated conditions are more likely to engage in behaviors that result in incarceration. Homelessness, substance abuse, and other social issues frequently intersect with mental health and crime, highlighting the need for preventative measures and better access to care. Addressing these systemic issues through mental health services could reduce the reliance on prisons as a default solution for managing individuals with complex needs.

On the other hand, there is concern that mental institutions may be used as a loophole for avoiding accountability, particularly in cases where offenders feign mental illness to escape harsher penalties. This perception has fueled skepticism about the efficacy of mental health-based interventions for certain types of crimes, particularly violent ones. Balancing the need for justice with the recognition that mental illness can impair judgment and behavior is a challenge that requires careful evaluation of each individual case.

Ultimately, the roles of mental institutions and the penal system should complement each other, rather than exist in opposition. Mental institutions are best suited for addressing the root causes of criminal behavior in individuals with genuine mental health conditions, providing treatment that can reduce the risk of future violence. The penal system, while necessary for ensuring public safety and holding offenders accountable, should incorporate more robust mental health services to address the needs of incarcerated individuals. A more integrated approach, combining elements of treatment, rehabilitation, and accountability, offers the best chance for reducing recidivism and improving outcomes for both offenders and society as a whole. By recognizing the strengths and limitations of each system, policymakers can work toward a more balanced and effective framework for addressing crime and mental illness.

# Chapter 14: Preventing the Next Monster

## Red Flags and Early Interventions to Stop Potential Serial Killers

Preventing the emergence of future serial killers hinges on identifying red flags early and implementing targeted interventions that address underlying behavioral, psychological, and environmental factors. While predicting violent behavior with absolute certainty is challenging, understanding common warning signs and risk factors can significantly improve prevention efforts. By recognizing these indicators early, families, educators, mental health professionals, and law enforcement can intervene before troubling behaviors escalate into violent acts.

One of the most well-known sets of red flags is the "Macdonald Triad," which includes a history of bedwetting beyond an appropriate age, cruelty to animals, and fire-setting behaviors. While the presence of these behaviors does not guarantee a future of violent crime, they often signal deep psychological distress, emotional dysregulation, or a lack of empathy—traits commonly found in serial offenders. Early intervention for children exhibiting these behaviors is critical, involving assessments by mental health professionals to understand the underlying issues and provide appropriate therapeutic support.

Chronic antisocial behavior, including persistent lying, stealing, bullying, and defiance toward authority figures, can also be indicative of deeper problems. Such behaviors are often symptomatic of conduct disorder, which, if left untreated, can evolve into antisocial personality disorder in adulthood—a condition frequently observed in serial killers. Addressing conduct disorder through behavioral therapy, family counseling, and educational support can redirect at-risk youth toward healthier social interactions and coping mechanisms.

Another significant red flag is a fascination with violence, particularly when coupled with a lack of empathy. Children or adolescents who derive pleasure from watching others suffer, or who display an unusual interest in graphic depictions of violence without the emotional discomfort typically associated with such content, warrant careful attention. This detachment from the suffering of others is a critical component of psychopathy. Early engagement through empathy training and supervised exposure to pro-social environments can help cultivate compassion and reduce violent impulses.

The role of trauma cannot be overlooked in the development of violent tendencies. Many serial killers report histories of severe physical, emotional, or sexual abuse. These traumatic experiences often contribute to feelings of powerlessness and rage, which can manifest in destructive behaviors. Identifying and supporting children who have experienced trauma is essential in breaking the cycle of violence. Trauma-informed therapy, such as cognitive-behavioral therapy (CBT) or eye movement desensitization and reprocessing (EMDR), can help individuals process their experiences, build resilience, and develop healthier ways of relating to others.

Isolation and social alienation are also significant factors. Individuals who struggle to form healthy relationships or who are consistently ostracized by peers are at greater risk of developing violent fantasies as a means of regaining control or asserting power. Programs that promote social skills development, mentorship, and inclusion can mitigate these risks by providing positive social experiences and reducing feelings of alienation.

Mental health conditions such as severe depression, schizophrenia, or personality disorders often intersect with violent behavior, especially when untreated. Early identification and consistent management of these conditions are crucial. Schools, pediatricians, and community programs should prioritize mental health screenings as part of routine evaluations, ensuring that at-risk individuals receive the support and treatment they need. Medication, therapy, and ongoing monitoring can significantly reduce the likelihood of violent behavior stemming from untreated mental illness.

Education and awareness play pivotal roles in prevention. Training teachers, counselors, and community members to recognize early warning signs and understand the importance of early intervention is essential. Educational programs that promote emotional literacy, conflict resolution, and empathy from a young age can foster environments where potential warning signs are addressed promptly and effectively. Encouraging open dialogue about mental health and behavioral concerns reduces stigma and encourages individuals to seek help before issues escalate.

Family dynamics also contribute significantly to the development of violent behavior. Dysfunctional family environments, characterized by neglect, abuse, or a lack of emotional support, can foster resentment and aggressive tendencies. Family therapy and parenting programs can equip caregivers with the skills needed to create supportive, nurturing environments. Providing parents and guardians with resources to address behavioral issues constructively can prevent the escalation of problematic behaviors.

Peer influence is another critical factor. Adolescents are particularly susceptible to the behaviors and attitudes of their peer groups. Associating with individuals who glorify violence or criminal behavior can reinforce negative tendencies. Conversely, positive peer influences can act as a protective factor, encouraging pro-social behavior and discouraging violence. Community and school-based programs that promote positive peer interactions and mentorship opportunities can redirect at-risk youth toward constructive activities.

The integration of technology into prevention strategies is increasingly important. With the rise of digital platforms, monitoring online behavior can provide insights into troubling patterns, such as obsessions with violent content or engagement in harmful online communities. While respecting privacy, developing tools that identify concerning behavior online can prompt early interventions and connect individuals with support systems before behaviors escalate.

Ultimately, preventing the next potential serial killer requires a multifaceted approach that combines early identification, mental health support, education, and community involvement. By addressing behavioral red flags with timely, compassionate, and evidence-based interventions, society can reduce the likelihood of future violence and foster healthier developmental pathways. Early intervention not only alters the trajectory of at-risk individuals but also contributes to the broader goal of creating safer, more resilient communities.

# The importance of mental health awareness and societal safeguard

The importance of mental health awareness and societal safeguards cannot be overstated in the effort to prevent violence and foster a healthier, more resilient society. Mental health plays a critical role in shaping how individuals process emotions, handle stress, and interact with others. When left unaddressed, mental health issues can contribute to destructive behaviors, broken relationships, and in extreme cases, violent acts. Raising awareness about mental health and implementing societal safeguards ensures that individuals receive the support they need, reducing stigma and preventing potential harm before it escalates.

Mental health awareness begins with education. Understanding the signs and symptoms of mental health conditions is essential for early detection and intervention. Many individuals who struggle with mental health issues suffer in silence, either because they are unaware of their condition or because societal stigma prevents them from seeking help. Public education campaigns, school programs, and workplace initiatives can teach people to recognize when they or someone they know might need support. Awareness helps normalize conversations about mental health, encouraging people to view it as just as important as physical health.

Early intervention is one of the most effective ways to address mental health challenges and prevent them from worsening. Mental health issues, such as depression, anxiety, and trauma-related disorders, often begin in childhood or adolescence. Schools, pediatricians, and community organizations play a vital role in identifying at-risk individuals and connecting them with resources. By addressing these issues early, society can mitigate long-term consequences and reduce the risk of harmful behaviors. Intervening at the right time can change the trajectory of an individual's life, steering them toward a path of healing and stability.

Societal safeguards are crucial in creating environments where mental health is prioritized and supported. This includes ensuring access to affordable and effective mental health care. Many individuals lack the financial means or insurance coverage to seek treatment, leaving their conditions untreated. Expanding access to therapy, counseling, and psychiatric services can bridge this gap, ensuring that no one is denied care due to socioeconomic barriers. Governments and private institutions alike have a responsibility to invest in mental health infrastructure, from funding community health centers to integrating mental health services into primary care settings.

Workplace mental health policies are another important safeguard. Employers who prioritize mental health not only support their employees but also contribute to a more productive and engaged workforce. Offering mental health benefits, providing flexible schedules, and fostering an open culture around mental health can make a significant difference in reducing stress and preventing burnout. When employees feel supported, they are more likely to seek help and less likely to experience crises that could have wider implications for themselves and others.

Community-based programs also play a significant role in fostering mental health awareness and safeguarding vulnerable populations. Initiatives such as crisis hotlines, peer support groups, and outreach programs provide immediate assistance and long-term support to individuals in need. These programs often serve as lifelines for those who feel isolated or overwhelmed, offering a safe space to share their experiences and access resources. Communities that prioritize mental health create a culture of care and empathy, reducing the stigma that often surrounds seeking help.

Another critical safeguard is the integration of mental health training into law enforcement, education, and healthcare systems. Police officers, teachers, and medical professionals are often the first to encounter individuals in mental health crises. Providing them with the training to recognize and respond appropriately to these situations can prevent escalation and ensure that individuals receive the care they need. For example, law enforcement agencies that implement crisis intervention teams (CIT) report better outcomes when dealing with individuals experiencing mental health emergencies, reducing the risk of harm to both the individual and the community.

Awareness and safeguards also extend to addressing societal factors that exacerbate mental health issues. Poverty, discrimination, social isolation, and lack of access to education are all stressors that can contribute to poor mental health. Tackling these systemic issues is essential for creating a society where mental health is valued and protected. Policies that promote social equity, affordable housing, and access to education are not just economic or political measures—they are investments in the mental well-being of the population.

The role of technology in mental health awareness is growing, offering both opportunities and challenges. Digital platforms provide access to teletherapy, mental health apps, and online support communities, making resources more accessible to those who might otherwise struggle to find help. However, technology can also contribute to mental health issues, particularly when it comes to cyberbullying, social media pressures, and the spread of harmful content. Striking a balance between leveraging technology for mental health support and protecting individuals from its negative effects is an ongoing challenge that requires careful oversight.

Ultimately, the importance of mental health awareness and societal safeguards lies in their ability to prevent suffering and promote a higher quality of life. By normalizing mental health conversations, expanding access to care, and addressing systemic inequalities, society can create an environment where individuals feel supported and empowered to seek help. This proactive approach benefits not only those struggling with mental health issues but also the broader community, fostering a culture of compassion, understanding, and resilience.

## Collaboration between psychology, law enforcement, and communities

Collaboration between psychology, law enforcement, and communities is essential in addressing and preventing violent crimes, particularly those involving serial offenders. Each of these sectors brings unique expertise and resources to the table, and their combined efforts create a comprehensive approach to understanding, investigating, and mitigating criminal behavior. By working together, psychologists, law enforcement agencies, and community members can bridge the gaps that often hinder effective crime prevention and resolution.

Psychology plays a vital role in analyzing the behavior and motivations of criminals. Forensic psychologists provide law enforcement with critical insights into the minds of offenders, helping to develop profiles that predict behavior, identify patterns, and narrow suspect pools. Behavioral analysis, for instance, can determine whether a series of crimes is linked to a single individual and shed light on the psychological drivers behind the actions. This understanding allows law enforcement to anticipate the offender's next move and adjust their investigative strategies accordingly. Psychologists also assist during interrogations by advising on techniques to elicit confessions or gain cooperation from suspects, tailoring approaches to the individual's psychological profile.

Law enforcement agencies contribute their investigative expertise, resources, and authority to address crime at the operational level. Police officers and detectives gather evidence, track suspects, and ensure public safety, while relying on psychological input to inform their tactics. Collaborative training programs, such as those focused on crisis intervention or de-escalation, equip officers with the skills needed to handle situations involving individuals with mental health challenges. When law enforcement adopts a trauma-informed approach guided by psychological principles, it reduces the risk of harm and increases the likelihood of a peaceful resolution.

Communities play an equally important role by serving as the eyes and ears on the ground. Residents are often the first to notice suspicious behavior or patterns that may indicate criminal activity. Building trust between law enforcement and communities fosters open communication, encouraging individuals to share information that could be crucial to investigations. Community members also provide vital context about local dynamics, helping law enforcement understand the unique challenges and vulnerabilities in specific areas.

Neighborhood watch programs, community policing initiatives, and public awareness campaigns strengthen these partnerships, creating a united front against crime.

Collaboration between these groups is particularly important in preventing violence. Psychologists can identify early warning signs of violent tendencies, such as antisocial behavior or untreated mental health conditions, and share this knowledge with educators, community leaders, and law enforcement. Communities, in turn, can implement programs that promote mental health awareness, conflict resolution, and social inclusion, addressing the root causes of violence before they escalate. Law enforcement can support these efforts by connecting at-risk individuals with resources and monitoring situations that may require intervention.

One of the most effective examples of this collaboration is the development of multidisciplinary task forces. These teams, composed of psychologists, police officers, social workers, and community advocates, work together to address complex cases involving serial crimes or threats to public safety. By pooling their expertise, they create a holistic approach that considers the psychological, social, and logistical aspects of criminal behavior. For instance, a task force investigating a series of murders might rely on psychological profiling to understand the offender's motives, community input to identify potential leads, and police resources to track and apprehend the suspect.

Education and training are also key components of successful collaboration. Law enforcement officers benefit from training sessions led by psychologists on topics such as understanding trauma, recognizing signs of mental illness, and using non-confrontational communication techniques. Similarly, community leaders and residents can be educated about how to spot warning signs, report suspicious activity, and support individuals at risk of engaging in criminal behavior. These educational efforts foster a shared sense of responsibility and equip all parties with the tools needed to contribute effectively to crime prevention.

Collaboration also extends to post-crime efforts, such as rehabilitation and community rebuilding. Psychologists can guide offenders through treatment programs aimed at reducing recidivism, while law enforcement ensures that public safety is maintained during the reintegration process. Communities play a role in supporting both victims and offenders, creating environments that promote healing and reintegration rather than perpetuating cycles of violence. When all three sectors work together, they create a support network that addresses the needs of victims, holds offenders accountable, and fosters long-term safety and stability.

Ultimately, the collaboration between psychology, law enforcement, and communities is about creating a unified strategy to address crime comprehensively. By combining psychological insights, investigative expertise, and community engagement, this partnership tackles crime at its roots, ensures effective responses, and builds trust among all stakeholders. This integrated approach not only improves public safety but also strengthens the social fabric, fostering a culture of cooperation, understanding, and resilience.

# Conclusion: Reflections on the Human Psyche

## What Serial Killers Teach Us

Serial killers reveal unsettling truths about the human psyche, exposing the darkest corners of our nature where empathy, morality, and restraint fail to exist. Their actions force us to confront the thin line between normalcy and deviance, challenging the belief that evil is easily recognizable or confined to certain individuals. Through their crimes, serial killers highlight the extremes of human behavior, where a combination of psychological, biological, and environmental factors can culminate in acts of unimaginable violence. They are both products of their circumstances and perpetrators of chaos, serving as reminders of the complex interplay between nature and nurture.

The ongoing fascination with serial killers stems from their ability to evoke both fear and intrigue. They disrupt the ordinary, violating the boundaries of safety and trust that society relies on to function. This fascination often lies in their duality—the ability to appear charming, intelligent, or ordinary while harboring violent compulsions. People are drawn to the mystery of what drives someone to such acts, seeking to understand how a person can descend into such darkness. At the same time, serial killers embody the fears of random, senseless violence, reminding us of our own vulnerability. The media's portrayal of these individuals as enigmatic figures further fuels this interest, turning them into cultural symbols of fear and intrigue.

Understanding the minds of serial killers is not just an academic exercise; it holds real-world implications for protecting society. By studying their behavior, psychology, and methods, researchers and law enforcement gain insights into the warning signs, patterns, and triggers that lead to violent acts. Profiling techniques, forensic psychology, and behavioral analysis have all emerged from this effort, providing critical tools for identifying and apprehending offenders before they can strike again. This knowledge also informs early intervention strategies, helping to address the factors that contribute to violent behavior, such as childhood trauma, mental illness, or social isolation. Through understanding the minds of these "monsters," society can develop better systems for prevention, detection, and rehabilitation.

Serial killers challenge us to reflect on humanity's capacity for both darkness and resilience. They reveal the fragility of societal structures and the importance of vigilance, empathy, and accountability. While their actions represent the worst of human behavior, the response to their crimes—through community solidarity, advancements in criminal justice, and psychological research—shows humanity's ability to confront and overcome even the most harrowing challenges. In studying the minds of serial killers, we gain not only the tools to combat violence but also a deeper understanding of the factors that shape human behavior, reminding us of the importance of compassion, awareness, and collective responsibility in building a safer world.

# References

Here are some authoritative references that can support the research and credibility of The Psychology of Serial Killers: Inside the Mind of Monsters and Patterns of Predation. These sources include books, academic papers, and forensic psychology studies related to serial killers, criminal profiling, and behavioral analysis.

Books:
Douglas, John E., & Olshaker, Mark. (1995). Mindhunter: Inside the FBI's Elite Serial Crime Unit. Scribner.

A foundational book on criminal profiling by a former FBI agent who pioneered behavioral analysis.
Ressler, Robert K., & Shachtman, Tom. (1992). Whoever Fights Monsters: My Twenty Years Tracking Serial Killers for the FBI. St. Martin's Press.

Provides firsthand insights from one of the earliest criminal profilers.
Hickey, Eric W. (2015). Serial Murderers and Their Victims (7th Edition). Cengage Learning.

A comprehensive academic textbook analyzing serial killers and their behaviors.
Wilson, Colin, & Seaman, Donald. (2007). The Serial Killers: A Study in the Psychology of Violence. Skyhorse.

Examines famous serial killers and the psychological factors behind their crimes.
Vronsky, Peter. (2021). American Serial Killers: The Epidemic Years 1950-2000. Berkley Books.

A historical examination of serial killings in America and the societal factors contributing to them.
Schechter, Harold. (2003). The Serial Killer Files: The Who, What, Where, How, and Why of the World's Most Terrifying Murderers. Ballantine Books.

A detailed encyclopedia of infamous serial killers and their crimes.
Keppel, Robert D. (1997). Signature Killers. Pocket Books.

Analyzes the patterns and psychological signatures of notorious serial murderers.
Academic and Forensic Psychology Studies:
Kocsis, Richard N. (Ed.). (2007). Criminal Profiling: International Theory, Research, and Practice. Humana Press.

Examines criminal profiling methodologies from an academic perspective.
Hare, Robert D. (1999). Without Conscience: The Disturbing World of the Psychopaths Among Us. The Guilford Press.

Discusses psychopathy, a key trait in many serial killers, and its implications in criminal behavior.
Canter, David, & Youngs, Donna. (2009). Investigative Psychology: Offender Profiling and the Analysis of Criminal Action. Wiley.

Introduces scientific methods used in offender profiling and crime scene analysis.
Law Enforcement and FBI Reports:
Federal Bureau of Investigation (FBI). (2005). Serial Murder: Multi-Disciplinary Perspectives for Investigators. U.S. Department of Justice.

A detailed guide to understanding serial killers, their motivations, and investigative techniques.
Holmes, Ronald M., & Holmes, Stephen T. (2009). Profiling Violent Crimes: An Investigative Tool (5th Edition). SAGE Publications.

Covers the principles of behavioral profiling and its application in solving violent crimes.
Egger, Steven A. (2002). The Killers Among Us: An Examination of Serial Murder and Its Investigation (2nd Edition). Pearson.

Discusses investigative failures and improvements in tracking serial offenders.
Case Studies & Criminal Investigations:
Caputi, Jane. (1987). The Age of Sex Crime. Women's Press.

Analyzes the cultural and gender-related aspects of serial murder.
Newton, Michael. (2006). The Encyclopedia of Serial Killers (2nd Edition). Checkmark Books.

A detailed reference book covering hundreds of serial killers worldwide.
Simpson, Robert D. (2018). Forensic Psychology: The Science Behind Criminal Behavior. Springer.

Provides an academic approach to forensic psychology and criminal motivations.
These references provide a blend of real-world case studies, law enforcement perspectives, forensic psychological research, and criminological theory, helping to support the depth and

authenticity of The Psychology of Serial Killers: Inside the Mind of Monsters and Patterns of Predation.

# About the Author

Scott R. Vanderbilt is a criminologist, forensic psychologist, and acclaimed author known for his penetrating insights into the criminal mind and the darker aspects of human behavior. With a career spanning over two decades, Vanderbilt has worked alongside law enforcement agencies, behavioral analysts, and legal professionals to unravel some of the most complex cases involving serial offenders and violent crimes. His expertise in criminal profiling and behavioral analysis has earned him recognition as a leading voice in the fields of forensic psychology and criminology.

Born and raised in Chicago, Illinois, Vanderbilt grew up in an urban environment that sparked his early fascination with the intersection of psychology and crime. After earning a bachelor's degree in psychology, he pursued advanced studies in forensic psychology, obtaining his master's degree and PhD from Georgetown University. His groundbreaking research focused on the psychological and environmental factors contributing to violent criminal behavior, particularly in serial offenders. This work laid the foundation for his lifelong mission to understand the human psyche and the extremes to which it can descend.

Vanderbilt's professional career has been marked by a dedication to bridging the gap between theory and practice. He has served as a consultant on numerous high-profile criminal investigations, applying his expertise in behavioral profiling to aid in identifying and apprehending offenders. His contributions have been instrumental in the development of modern investigative techniques, including geographic profiling and the refinement of psychological assessments for violent offenders. Thornton's ability to analyze complex patterns of behavior has made him a sought-after advisor for law enforcement agencies across the globe.

In addition to his work in the field, Vanderbilt is a passionate educator and advocate for mental health awareness. He has lectured at prestigious universities, sharing his knowledge with the next generation of criminologists and psychologists. His advocacy extends to community programs aimed at early intervention and the prevention of violent behavior, reflecting his belief in addressing the root causes of crime through education and support.

Scott R. Vanderbilt's writing is characterized by its ability to distill complex psychological theories into compelling narratives that resonate with both professionals and general readers. His books, including The Psychology of Serial Killers: Inside the Mind of Monsters and Patterns of Predation, blend meticulous research with gripping storytelling, offering readers an in-depth exploration of the darkest corners of the human mind. Through his work, Vanderbilt invites readers to confront uncomfortable truths about human behavior while emphasizing the importance of understanding and prevention.

When he's not analyzing criminal behavior or writing his next book, Vanderbilt enjoys hiking in remote areas, where he finds solace in the tranquility of nature, a stark contrast to the disturbing realities he studies. He currently resides in Washington, D.C., with his two rescue dogs, Marlow and Poe, who are named after literary figures reflecting his love of psychological thrillers and classic literature.

Scott R. Vanderbilt remains committed to shedding light on the shadows of the human mind, offering insights that not only illuminate the complexities of criminal behavior but also inspire efforts to build a safer and more empathetic society.

# Disclaimer

The information presented in this book is for educational and informational purposes only and is not intended as professional advice. The author and publisher have made every effort to ensure the accuracy of the information; however, they assume no responsibility for errors, omissions, or any outcomes resulting from the application of the contents. Readers are encouraged to consult with a qualified professional for specific advice tailored to their situation.

All opinions expressed are those of the author and do not reflect the views of any affiliated organizations. The reader assumes all risks for the use of the material provided in this book. The author and publisher disclaim any liability for direct or indirect consequences arising from the use or interpretation of the information.

All rights reserved. No part of this book may be reproduced, distributed, or transmitted in any form without prior written permission from the author or publisher, except in the case of brief quotations used in reviews.

# Copyright

© 2025 by Scott R. Vanderbilt

All rights reserved.

No part of this book may be reproduced, distributed, or transmitted in any form or by any means, including photocopying, recording, or other electronic or mechanical methods, without the prior written permission of the publisher, except in the case of brief quotations embodied in critical reviews and certain other noncommercial uses permitted by copyright law.

This book is a work of fiction/nonfiction. Names, characters, places, and incidents are products of the author's imagination or used fictitiously. Any resemblance to actual events, locales, or persons, living or dead, is purely coincidental.

Printed in the United States of America

## Legal Notice

This book is for informational and educational purposes only. While the author and publisher have made every effort to provide accurate and up-to-date information, they assume no responsibility for any errors, inaccuracies, or omissions. Any reliance placed on the information in this book is strictly at the reader's discretion and risk.

The content is not intended to replace professional advice, including but not limited to medical, legal, financial, or other professional services. Readers should consult with an appropriate professional for specific guidance related to their unique circumstances.

All trademarks, product names, and company names mentioned herein are the property of their respective owners. Their inclusion does not imply endorsement, affiliation, or sponsorship. Unauthorized reproduction, distribution, or transmission of this publication in any form is prohibited without prior written consent from the author or publisher.

By reading this book, you agree to indemnify and hold harmless the author, publisher, and any affiliated parties from and against all claims, liabilities, losses, or damages resulting from your use of the information provided.